STARTING TO TEACH

STARTING TO TEACH

Surviving and Succeeding in the Classroom

— **Anthony D Smith** —

Books for Teachers
Series Editor: Tom Marjoram

KOGAN PAGE

First published in 1988 by Kogan Page Ltd,
120 Pentonville Road, London N1 9JN

Reprinted 1990

British Library Cataloguing in Publication Data
Smith, Anthony D
    Starting to teach: surviving and
    succeeding in the classroom.—
    —(Kogan Page books for teachers series).
    1. Teaching—Manuals.
    I. Title
    371.1'02
    ISBN 1-85091-582-2

Printed and bound in Great Britain by
Biddles Ltd, Guildford and King's Lynn

CONTENTS

4
Assessing Progress and Coping with the Paperwork

5
Achieving Job Satisfaction Through Relations with Students, Colleagues and the Outside World

Acknowledgement

I would like to thank Mr Tom Marjoram for providing the illustrations in this book and for giving me valuable advice in the preparation of the text.

Dedication

To my parents and teaching colleagues.

Introduction

The Enthusiastic Teacher – Why this Book Needed to be Written

Not many of you should presume to be teachers, my brothers, because you know that we who teach will be judged more strictly.

The Bible: James 3.1

Starting to teach brings you into a whole new world of human relationships. The new teacher is faced by rapid changes in the educational world, which reflect shifts in the attitudes of society itself. There seems to be little to cling to as we launch into a new career, yet we seek some reassurance that we shall be proficient, effective and fruitful in our teaching.

If you have been teacher-trained, you should have the basic theoretical knowledge and practical skills, but you may not have been provided with the self-confidence you crave in your first few teaching years: confidence in your methods, your style, your whole approach to the learning process and what you are trying to do for your students as a good teacher.

For the untrained teacher, taking on part-time or temporary work for the first time, there is even more uncertainty because you do not have the confidence that, at least on paper, you are qualified to teach. You probably have a more than adequate command of your subject, but are concerned about your ability to 'put it over' to your students.

Now it is quite inevitable that the first few years will be traumatic and exhausting; it takes time to adjust to a new way of life. But this period need not also be totally confusing; the object of this book is to show how you can acquire a teaching style of your own over a relatively short time, avoiding many of the mistakes that seem inevitable in the gaining of experience 'the hard way'.

If you consider yourself an experienced teacher, I hope that some of what I say will confirm that experience, and offer you some encouragement. After a few years in the profession, many teachers find it difficult not to become stale; they lose their initial enthusiasm. Of course, we cannot retain that idealistic vision we may have held when we first entered teaching, but I have tried to provide words of consolation to teachers who may be asking themselves whether the community appreciates their efforts.

This book tries to show you what successful teaching involves. If there's one word I would use to sum up what a teacher needs, it's *enthusiasm*. Someone who cannot communicate this quality is no teacher in my book, indeed I was going to call this book 'The Enthusiastic Teacher'. Most of us can recall teachers who were able to transmit their enthusiasm for their subject to us, to stir us, to arouse an independent desire to know or do more. I would submit that this quality lies at the very heart of all successful teaching.

Consider the great religious teachers from history. They gathered disciples around them because they were able to communicate enthusiasm; it was caught rather than taught, and their ideas have been passed down the generations in the same way. Enthusiasm is a very personal quality, a living quality, because we, the teachers, are ourselves still learning, and this is why it is so difficult to teach people to be good teachers. You need to develop a variety of talents for teaching, but the talent for putting across your own enthusiasm is perhaps the most valuable of all.

These days, there are few people who go into education for the money or job prospects, so we can take it that most would-be teachers contemplate the profession because they feel they have something to offer. I believe that the most valuable thing they have to offer is their enthusiasm: their ardent zeal to share knowledge, to pass on skills; this is at the core of the teaching process, and is what makes teaching a vocation.

It's all very well to say you have a vocation, but that doesn't make you an effective teacher. You need to harness your enthusiasm: to concentrate it into the most productive channels, and this needs a lot of hard work on your part. Whether you are a new teacher or just seeking a little inspiration for your accepted vocation, this book is designed to help you with the task. Basically, it involves:

1. Providing the framework of discipline
2. Organizing the classroom and planning your lessons
3. Achieving student-centred learning
4. Assessing progress and coping with paperwork
5. Achieving job satisfaction through relations with students, colleagues and the outside world.

Teaching can be such an interesting career because there is so much variety. Outsiders wonder how this can be, because it appears to be the repetition of a fixed collection of knowledge and skills by standardized methods to relatively homogeneous groups of students. Well, first, knowledge and skills are changing faster than ever before; no teacher can sit back and think that he or she 'knows it all'. Second, teaching and assessment methods are in a state of flux, as we seek the most appropriate methods for our current social, technological and economic circumstances. Thirdly – and this has always been the case – each group of students presents a unique set of challenges to the teacher. There's no substitute for the experience that is gained by coming to grips with the learning problems of individual students; what this book attempts to do is to provide a down-to-earth guide for all who aspire to achieve success with their students' learning. There is tremendous job satisfaction to be gained from facilitating learning; this is the reward that awaits the new teacher who is starting to teach.

Chapter 1

Providing the Framework of Discipline

He who looks for trouble will most certainly find it.
An old Chinese proverb, of doubtful authenticity!

First Impressions

I claim no originality for the techniques suggested here; it just seems to me that it would be better if inexperienced teachers could be aware of them before embarking on their career, rather than having to learn by painful mistakes. It will be difficult to apply these techniques at first, but experience usually confirms their wisdom.

Your students will judge you by what you do, as well as what you say. It's difficult to live a lie, so if you appear to them outside the classroom as disillusioned, cynical and having no particular set of values which give purpose to your life, you can hardly expect them to accept your enthusiastic performances in the classroom as genuine. Remember that 'discipline' comes from the same Latin root as 'disciple'. A disciple is a follower of a master who sets an example; we still refer to 'schoolmasters'. Although the word 'discipline' has become debased to mean the maintenance of order, it is no bad thing to consider the original meaning, and resolve that in our teaching we will endeavour to get our students to follow our example of self-discipline.

Teaching, as generally understood, involves some sort of encounter between teacher and student; in most cases there is a formal pattern of encounters at set times over the duration of the course. The *first encounter* is tremendously important; although the students may have had previous meetings with you and may have been conditioned to some extent by the general atmosphere of the institution in which classes are held, the actual start of the educational process so far as you and they are concerned is to be *now*.

Your Appearance

First impressions count. Everyone judges from appearances in the absence of other criteria, so if you want to make the best of this moment, make your appearance appropriate for the class – it can set the tone. If you want a relaxed atmosphere for an evening class for mature students, dress casually. If you are teaching for professional examinations, dress in the manner appropriate to that profession. If you are teaching less mature students, a compromise between comfort and formality is usually sought, but remember that a more formal appearance generally helps in the maintenance of discipline – it instils a certain respect. When we visit our doctor or solicitor, we feel let down if they are casually dressed – it's nonsense of course, they're the same person underneath, but somehow we can't convince ourselves that they have the same authority in casual clothes, and this applies for most teachers. (I use the word 'most' advisedly, since I would be the first to admit that, as in most walks of life, there are good teachers who break nearly all the rules; they usually have talent to spare, a blessing which is not available to most of us.) One very practical point: black or navy are unsuitable colours for teachers' clothes if they are using chalk; I was delighted with my new navy blazer until I started boardwork – within a short time I had to abandon the garment in favour of my usual grey or beige outfits.

MAKING YOUR ENTRANCE

Right, so you are dressed for the part; but to use a theatrical analogy, you now have to make your entrance. The first entrance is of course the most important, but remember that every entrance you make into a classroom should be significant. It goes without saying that you should turn up on time – if you arrive late, not only will your performance be affected by your being flustered, but you will also find it very difficult to achieve subsequent discipline as regards student lateness. Allow adequate time to get down the corridor that first time in case you are waylaid by a colleague; you can take a few deep breaths as you go in if you are feeling tense – I still feel a bit that way when going to see a class for the first time.

When you enter, do so in a positive authoritative way; hold your head high, do not smile, but try to appear confident. Do not be stopped by a student at the door, or be drawn into immediate conversation with students near your table, as this spoils the effect, but aim straight for your table and deposit your teaching file on it. If there is a dirty chalkboard or other distracting display, deal with this before facing the class. Now stand still and look slowly around the room, trying to make eye contact with as many students as possible. Usually, the students will be waiting expectantly, not knowing what to make of you at this stage – they are waiting for a cue from you. This is the time to start the two-way process that is teaching/learning, so introduce yourself. Whether the students are on first name terms with you depends on the average age of the class and the custom of the institution, but as a general rule it's best to start on a formal basis and relax later, as one would do in normal social encounters. 'Sir' and 'Miss' are getting a bit dated now, but you should insist on your students taking the trouble to address you properly, so write your name on the board to help them remember; they can refer to it during the first lesson. (Having the commonest British surname, I have a distinct advantage here!)

Disciplinary Guidelines

The order in which you proceed from here is a matter of personal taste, but I like to lay down my disciplinary guidelines at this stage. Discipline is so central to education that I have devoted this whole chapter to it, and I would advise you to spell out quite clearly during the first class the kind of behaviour you expect and what you will not put up with. The more mature and responsible your students, the less emphasis you need to put on this – it becomes a matter of saying something like, 'I'm sure I don't need to remind you of the need for punctuality in attending classes and handing in written work . . . '. More mature students readily appreciate the rewards to be gained from a course through hard work; the less responsible have to be 'assisted' in this realization through a mixture of pressures and rewards and, I hope, the picking up of a little of your enthusiasm, too.

Experienced teachers will tell you that you must start as you mean to carry on; you can gradually relax your strictness as you gain your students' respect and confidence, but you can never recover a position after discipline has been lost. This is sound advice. Teachers who say, 'I'm going to read the Riot Act to that class!' have already lost the battle unless that is their first lesson. If there is any possibility of discipline problems arising with a class, I do my Riot Act performance at the first lesson. I have my copy of the 'Act' in my notes, so that I won't forget any of the vital points, and then I 'lay down the law' quite clearly. Some teachers also give a handout on this, so that offending students can't come back later (as some invariably do) and claim ignorance of your decrees. To my less mature and responsible students, I lay great emphasis on reliability – turning up punctually, handing in work on time and generally in maintaining a consistently good performance throughout the course.

TEACHING STYLE

Now, many new teachers will be aware of the way in which a so-called *'authoritarian'* teaching style is frowned upon by the teacher trainers. What I recommend may appear to fall into that category, but a strict approach is often mistaken for an authoritarian one. You can have an ordered approach to learning which is still student-centred; a *'democratic'* teaching style does not equate with 'anything goes'. Obviously, your actual style will be greatly influenced by your personality. For most new teachers, I think it is necessary for a certain amount of role-play to be carried out; you have to act the part of the strict teacher whether it comes naturally or not. There are two common reactions from teachers faced with their first classes: they either try to be too familiar with their students in order to gain some cooperation from them, or they withdraw into their subject and end up teaching that rather than their students. Both these approaches are mistaken, and will eventually lose your students' respect. You need to *gain* that respect, so that you will be able to initiate and supervise the methods of activity-based learning I propose. Your personality will then be able to blossom through your teaching style, and your discipline problems should be reduced to manageable proportions.

PUNCTUALITY

Let us consider more of the detail of discipline. Punctuality is an awful headache for teachers. Lack of it is a form of indiscipline, and must be tackled at the outset. Again, it generally pays to be very strict to start with, but you must be realistic – you can only lay down that students arrive as promptly as is humanly possible. At the first class, it's not usually possible to do much about late arrivals, as new students may not be familiar with the building or may be delayed by administrative matters. The time to enforce discipline on punctuality is at the second lesson and this will be covered once we have got through the first lesson! For the time being, state clearly the behaviour you expect and try to demonstrate your determination to follow up your words with action.

SANCTIONS

The sanctions you have available should be spelt out now – not left to later when discipline is breaking down. Sanctions will vary according to institution, but vague threats are useless. For instance, nearly all colleges reserve the right to expel students, after the appropriate disciplinary procedure. I tell my students that if one of them disrupts the class and adversely affects other students' learning, I will have no hesitation in recommending that the student be asked to leave, and I mention that on a number of occasions I have actually done this. I also point out that a good college reference is a valuable asset when job seeking and if a student's contribution is nil or even negative, I shall see that his or her reference says so. These may be strong words, but if you don't nail your colours to the mast at the outset, you will find that the water becomes very choppy later on! I shall return to the legal basis of sanctions later in this chapter.

PREVENTING DISRUPTIVE BEHAVIOUR

While you are making your position crystal clear, keep a close watch on the students' reactions. If any student shows unmistakable signs of being unwilling to accept your rules, or does anything disruptive, pick this up immediately and give a firm, controlled, verbal rebuke, addressing the student by name. (If you don't know his or her name, ask.) This is to act as a warning to the rest of the class and can work wonders in avoiding the need for later, more exhausting and less effective disciplinary action. It's a bit unfair on the student concerned if he or she had no real intention of actually being disruptive, but good can flow from it if all students are made aware that you are not going to stand any nonsense. One year, I noticed one student in his first class casually sitting back, so I sternly asked him to sit up straight. The effect was amazing, as the whole row of students suddenly straightened themselves – like a reverse domino effect!

Seating Arrangements

A word now about where students sit in the classroom. I have come to the conclusion that control over the seating of students is more important than most teachers realize, and I shall have more to say about classroom organization in Chapter 2. The chances are that the students who wish to avoid your disciplinary control will sit as far away as possible, with several rows of desks between you and them as a form of 'defence'. It's surprising how many teachers seem meekly to accept this. Although I would only direct individual students to sit in the front row, say, if there was a serious discipline problem with those particular students, I do feel that the teacher should have the last word on seating arrangements. Once again, if you start off insisting on your wishes, you are more likely to be successful. How many classrooms have you passed where there is a large gap between teacher and students, with rows of empty intervening desks? Or have you had to endure the aggravation of teaching two groups of students clustered at opposite sides of the room, so that while your attention is directed to one group, the other does as it pleases? The answer here is to ensure that students sit in a suitable layout, together, and near the teacher. It is possible for the teacher to move towards the students if they are all grouped towards the back of the room, but it is far better if you get them to come forward to you. This needs some applied psychology; you don't want your requests to be defied and cause a confrontation, with possible loss of face for you. Make your wishes known in a firm but courteous way, expecting compliance in a brisk, but not brusque, manner. If you show that you mean business, students will usually, reluctantly, agree to move, but you may need to cajole them by explaining that the layout is needed for group work or other class activity. Once the students are used to moving at your behest, you will find it much easier to organize classroom activities which need different layouts, but which often fail in the hands of inexperienced teachers because they do not have the courage to ask students to move. Above all, taking control of this vital matter from the outset stamps your authority on the class and helps discipline considerably.

Outline Your Career

I usually end this part of my performance by telling new students a bit about myself. I don't go into personal details which are only appropriate for discussion on a one-to-one basis such as when you are counselling a student. I simply give a broad outline of my education, training and experience. If you have held responsible positions in the past, it does no harm to mention them, provided you realize that you are doing this to gain students' respect, not their admiration. If you are new to teaching, don't mention this fact; deflect all questions about your personal life and about how long you have 'been in teaching'. Fend off really persistent students with replies which are courteous and good-natured, but which make it quite clear that you are not going to answer questions on personal matters. As you get to know your students, they will also get to know more about you; this is natural and healthy. To begin with, however, make sure that *you* decide who asks the questions!

Get to Know Your Students

Having given your students their disciplinary guidelines, you can then hand out the course programme, explain it and discuss any queries which arise. At this stage you must get to know your students so that two-way communication can begin. I like to pass round a sheet of paper to collect names – this not only provides a ready-made class list, but also gives a sample of students' handwriting which is often useful for tracing the authors of anonymous work handed in. It's very helpful to let each student introduce him or herself and just ask them one or two questions. Always be on your guard when speaking to one student that you have not lost the others' attention – maintain their interest by eye contact and by turning to other students to ask for their comments on some matter that arises during these 'chats'. Be careful not to put any students 'on the spot' or embarrass them. If things become awkward with a particular student, pass on rapidly to the next. Of course, if a student becomes abusive or insolent, you must administer an appropriate rebuke as I have suggested, but it's not always easy to know whether a new student is being deliberately disruptive or is just reacting to what he or she perceives to be a threatening situation. When in doubt, you can't beat the 'see me afterwards' technique; this lets the other students know that you are not prepared to overlook the incident, but gives the student the chance to explain him or herself privately and an amicable resolution of the difficulty to be achieved.

If you have access to students' papers giving details of their background, it's worth glancing at them before meeting the class, and then studying the papers in more detail after two or three weeks, when you are able to put faces to the names on the papers. Knowledge of students' outside interests, eg sport, may help you get to know them more quickly, and can assist with the problem of motivation. Sometimes a student has some special feature which he or she is reluctant to reveal, but knowledge of which may help you assist the student, for example some physical or mental handicap. Being aware of this can avoid embarrassing moments, such as when I was chiding a student for periodic absences, only to be informed by him in front of the class that these were due to attacks of epilepsy.

Ending the Class

Finally, before the class ends, make sure your timetable and theirs coincide! Don't end the class early, or they'll always expect this. State clearly what is going to be tackled in the next lesson and what books or equipment the students need to bring along. Remind them about turning up punctually and finish the class positively, on an upbeat note, looking forward to next time. Always aim to be in full control at the end; don't let students dictate to you when to end the lesson by putting their files away before you have finished – make it clear to them that the learning process ends when *you* say so. The students will then go away with the impression that you were in full control throughout – which may or may not have been the case!

Student Motivation

If you set your standards when you meet a new group for the first time, you must then build on that foundation. This is something to which you may have to give much attention for the entire duration of the course. One of the fundamental problems you will continually encounter is that of motivation. If only your students really wanted to learn, your task would be so much easier! Problems of discipline and motivation tend to go together; a well-motivated class may still find learning difficult, but at least your efforts are not continually diverted into keeping order and trying to stir students out of their lethargy, indifference, or even outright hostility.

THE EFFECT OF CHANGING SOCIAL ATTITUDES

Like education itself, motivation manifests itself by the behaviour it brings forth. Attitudes of society in general, and young people in particular, are changing rapidly; typically, your students may ask 'Why do we have to do this?'. Young people no longer accept what is taught without question, and perhaps this is a good thing. What is not good is the tendency of many young people, especially the low achievers, to reject the present education and training set-up as having little relevance to their needs. As teachers, we can at least recognize the existence and strength of these negative motivational attitudes, and do what we can to counter them. Unless we are dealing with very young children, we face students who may have already acquired such negative attitudes from family, friends and the general environment.

THE NEED TO STIMULATE MOTIVATION

New teachers are often puzzled by students' lack of motivation in the educational and training context, because it seems to be abundantly present in other areas of students' lives; consider the enthusiasm for pop music and sport. Obviously, we cannot compete on the same terms, and nor would we wish to, because we are offering something which we hope will be of more permanent value. However, we cannot live in ivory towers, so what we do in the classroom – or rather what our students do – should stimulate motivation. How is this done? Well, to some extent we can tap those areas which do seem to motivate students, but I would be cautious about taking this too far; you cannot make pop music the vehicle for all education! No, I think that the new teacher should be aware of both what affects motivation and how it can be stimulated.

LESSON PRESENTATION

What do unmotivated students say? 'This is boring!' What does this mean? It means that the students are not being stimulated as individuals. Now I would agree that it is not our job to make life more interesting than it really is; we know that large stretches of it are just boring routine, but we can at least take a leaf out of the book of the media producers of the pop culture, and present our product more attractively. Even then, our enticingly packaged lesson may still be rejected, due to the ingrained negative attitudes mentioned above. One method of overcoming these is to try to get to know your students as people, so that you can understand better their individual motivation. I know this isn't easy with a large class, but in my experience your effort to do this will be appreciated by the students. Note that I don't recommend becoming too familiar with students; what you should do is make every effort to treat them as individuals, and the first step along that road is to memorize their names. I return to this later in the chapter.

COMPETITION

Another useful means of motivation is competition. Most of our educational system has been based on it, to the detriment of the low achievers. If a student believes he or she has little chance of 'success', motivation is killed, and the students regard themselves as the rejects of society. In this sense, then, competition produces some negative results, but it can be used for more positive purposes in the classroom. We can adapt the exciting competitive aspects of sport to encourage participation in games and role-plays which may arrest our students' interest. Try to use quizzes or skills competitions to assess progress and carry further the learning process. Any form of *active* learning is preferable to the passive type; I shall return to activity-based, student-centred learning in Chapter 3.

SET CLEAR AIMS

The setting of clear aims or goals also helps to maintain interest. We all know how you can keep walking just a bit further if your destination is in view. Try to be clear about your aims, and make sure these are communicated effectively to your students. The trouble with not giving low achievers any qualifications to aspire to is that this removes a major incentive to learn. Fortunately, new examinations are being designed to cater for their needs, and thus provide some focus for their studies. If you are not affected by these, it is still vital to set some aims; a good way is through the course programme, to which I shall return in Chapter 2. However, you can still encourage your students to aim for something by rewarding their efforts. The more cynical students may not respond to verbal reward, but many students will work better if they are given immediate praise for their efforts; this has a much better effect than the negative 'telling off' of students. I deal with 'positive reinforcement' in Chapter 3. The carrot and stick technique has proved its worth over the ages; provide plenty of carrots and keep the stick in reserve!

THE PSYCHOLOGICAL APPROACH

The last of our means of motivation should be based upon our knowledge of the psychology of our students. This of course depends upon the age group we are dealing with, but for older children and young people we need to be aware that they will wish to be seen as persons who matter and have their own individuality. It is therefore important for teachers having disciplinary problems with certain students to look behind the bad behaviour at the individuals concerned, and see if there is an identifiable cause of the wrongdoing. This is best done in consultation with the course tutor, and can of course be very time-consuming, but it may help you to deal with some very 'difficult' students. Repression of these students by authoritarian measures is most unlikely to be successful; try to help them as individuals without making the other students think you are 'going easy' on them. It may be a good idea to encourage them by giving them some sort of responsibility, such as making them team leaders, provided this doesn't appear to be a reward for their waywardness. Giving such attention to difficult students often pays dividends, but never forget that you are responsible for the learning of the whole class, so use this technique with discretion.

LOSS OF MOTIVATION IN ADOLESCENCE

Why do many students seem to lose their motivation as they move into their teens? Some will already be losing interest as they experience failure at school, and feel that they have nothing to aim for, apart from getting out of the education system. Young people will wish to assert their independence, which is enhanced if they take on evening or weekend jobs and have money to spend. Most will be distracted by the physiological and emotional changes of adolescence. Perhaps more than anything else, the attitudes of young people will be coloured by adult society's expectations of their behaviour. We tend to look for trouble, and interpret all youthful behaviour as a threat to our settled, adult world. 'He who looks for trouble will most certainly find it', says the proverb, so we ought to look for the positive side of our students' behaviour.

I hope that these remarks will have demonstrated how vital it is to understand the motivation behind your students, or even the lack of it. Increasingly, teachers are having to encourage that motivation in order that learning can take place. Sometimes it's hard enough to motivate ourselves! If you can get your students interested and motivated, discipline problems tend to melt away. I don't espouse an approach which amounts to pandering to students' every whim and letting them tell you what to do; on the contrary, you should start off strictly, and gradually gain their confidence and cooperation, while demonstrating that you have something to offer them that *they* judge to be of value.

Lateness

The second lesson is the time to put into effect your plan for dealing with lateness. To some extent this is a personal matter; teachers have different ideas of the seriousness of different types of misdemeanours. Again, lateness is widely tolerated in our social and leisure relationships. However, I would suggest that toleration of too much lateness leads to other, more serious types of indiscipline – after all, being late is the first form of indiscipline a student can exhibit! Furthermore, you will probably be under some form of legal obligation to keep a register of attendances; school registers may be used as evidence in court. Therefore, treat attendance records with care; be scrupulous in keeping them, and get them completed as early in the lesson as practicable, in accordance with your institution's rules.

You will have to approach lateness bearing in mind the maturity of your students and the physical circumstances of their attendance. Mature people with half a lifetime of poor time-keeping behind them won't change as a result of your remonstrations and they will probably be counter-productive. Students coming to evening classes after work may have every reason for lateness and again little good can come of cross examinations. Full-time students are rather different, yet there again, morning registration may be plagued by excuses about public transport. Try to avoid a long-running saga here. As soon as a pattern of lateness emerges, take the matter up with the course tutor or other teacher responsible for that student. If you are responsible, check independently the student's story about the trains or buses, and if they are as described try to get this officially recognized so that all students affected get a proper dispensation. You often find that it's the students who live just round the corner who have the worst 'back trouble' in the morning – can't get it off the mattress – so be firm with them.

Late arrival to other classes during the rest of the day must take the physical circumstances into account: students must get from A to B and they may have to attend to personal needs. What you want to stop is *deliberate* lateness brought about by students making use of your class time for their own leisure purposes, so make it clear that you'll stand no nonsense. I had given my usual 'Riot Act' reading during the first lesson for a particular group. At the next lesson, the following week, they crawled in three, four, even six minutes late for the post-lunchtime class. I made a firm stand there and then – there was no excuse for not being in class on time after lunch. They were rather taken aback, but the shock tactics worked and next week they were all in place when I arrived – on the dot, of course. Now inevitably there will be what I call 'slippage' during the year; gradually more flexibility can be permitted, so long as this does not deteriorate into licence; but again, starting off on the right footing is crucial.

The key to dealing with these problems, as indeed with all matters of discipline, is to be positive and fair. Make it clear from the word go that you expect a proper apology for lateness – not just a breezy, 'Sorry I'm late' but a respectful explanation for the lateness. If it involves a delicate matter of health or family, the student can see you afterwards. Impress on your students that you only expect the sort of explanation that a reasonable employee would feel obliged to offer his or her boss. If they are already in employment, they will have some idea of what this means; if not, dreaming up plausible excuses will be good practice for them!

Fairness comes into the picture when you are confronted with a procession of late students during the early minutes of your lesson. The class will notice how you grade the severity of your 'telling off' as the degree of lateness increases. If you're not careful, you will wear yourself out dealing with latecomers before the lesson has really got underway and create an unfavourable atmosphere for learning. Latecomers can be an awful distraction, which you don't want to emphasize. So once the lesson is underway, it's advisable to motion to latecomers to sit down with a request to see you at the end of the lesson. This minimizes the disruption and enables you to deal in an appropriate manner with the latecomer without the danger that the other students will judge you to have been unduly lenient with that particular student. Incidentally, if I'm teaching an evening class, say, where a certain amount of lateness seems inevitable, I try to put the main points of the early part of the lesson on the board, so that latecomers have a chance to pick up the threads of the lesson. Your aim throughout must be to avoid turning discipline into a class 'side-show' – the best discipline is hidden, unremarked, but accepted by all as being there to maintain the framework of the teaching and learning process.

Maintaining Discipline

I have described in detail how to handle your first encounter with a class. From then on, and having dealt with the lateness problem, your aim should be to create the best possible conditions for learning to take place. Teachers sometimes feel they must discourage any student behaviour which breaks the convention of passive, attentive silence. This is unrealistic in two senses. First, unless you are dealing with very mature and responsible students, you'll find it impossible to keep them quiet and 'well behaved' all the time. Second, most gatherings of people outside the classroom environment are not governed by such artificial conventions. Two-way communication, audience participation, personal involvement – these are some of the catch-phrases of the age and teachers ignore the outside world at their peril. Fortunately, these fashionable methods are ideal teaching strategies, so we should welcome their influence in our classrooms. However, they do entail a different approach to classroom discipline, but not, I hasten to add, an abandonment of it.

SELF-DISCIPLINE
Ultimately, we are trying to imbue our students with that priceless gift of self-discipline, since in the last analysis what should concern us is our students' learning rather than our teaching; and learning can only come about if students are sufficiently self-disciplined to will it. Self-discipline is a bit like religion – it's caught, not taught. Your example must help to underpin class discipline and encourage self-discipline. Try to avoid losing your self-control, ie your temper, in class. Controlled anger, put on sparingly to demonstrate strong disapproval, is valuable occasion-

ally. Uncontrolled displays of temper are unprofessional and you should always apologize afterwards to the individuals or class which witnesses them.

GAINING AND RETAINING CONTROL

Once again, quiet, firm control is the aim. Shouting at a class is hopeless, whether in anger or simply to make yourself heard. Make it clear from the outset that if you ask for quiet and complete attention, you expect to receive it. Be polite but firm when requesting students' attention – say 'May I have your attention please', and then patiently wait for your request to be complied with. You may have to repeat your request and call on named students for their attention. Don't be afraid to wait for complete silence, looking around the room to establish eye contact if possible. With more immature classes, you'll have to settle for relative quiet, and if for some reason the students are particularly restless, it may be advisable to start the lesson and wait for settling down afterwards. Don't try to shout over them, but use some ploy to attract their attention and start them off. This can simply be putting something on the board for them to copy – most students will get out pen and paper and start copying it as a sort of reflex action, and so the lesson can begin. Alternatively, you could get them to divide into groups for an exercise which you rapidly distribute or put on the board. You're trying to gain their attention and involve them in the learning process and sometimes they need quite a push!

During a lesson, there are some techniques which will help you retain control. Standing to address students gives you a more commanding position – it enables you to see them better and vice versa. Sitting behind a table is a less positive, more defensive position, which will make it harder to stamp your authority on the class. Sit down when you enter the classroom, then your rising to speak will have more effect. Sit down when you have set an exercise for the students or are giving them a short break, or when you are just too tired to stand up any longer!

When you stand, don't just remain at the front of the class behind your desk, but venture forth into the body of the class. This is difficult if there are solid rows of desks, but I sometimes remove a desk to enable me to move to and fro among the students. Again, this facilitates class control – you can gravitate towards those students who are potentially disruptive or are simply not paying sufficient attention. You can check that proper notes are being taken, or that any other student activity is being done properly, by judicious looking-over of shoulders and commenting as appropriate. Be careful not to fall into the trap of spending too much time with one group of students in one corner of the room. Some may require extra tuition or discipline, but if you are allocating too much of your time and presence to a few students, the remainder of the class may become restless and discipline problems may arise from previously placid quarters. Class time must be fairly evenly spread between students; the time for intensive extra tuition or discipline is after class.

Avoid having favourites. Of course some students have more attractive personalities than others, but we mustn't fall into the trap of appearing to favour some students at the expense of others. Students notice this very quickly and your authority will be undermined if you don't make every effort to appear fair to one and all. This must encompass all contacts with your students: question and answer and discussion sessions, marking, classroom discipline and contact outside class. If you let some students have favoured status, they may take advantage of this, causing resentment among other students and a loss of respect for you. It's just another facet of the good, professional teacher: he or she has no favourites.

Try to use students' names as often as possible. It's very hard to pull students up unless you can address them by their names. Some teachers draw a plan of the class; I used to do this, but now I prefer to work from a list of names obtained from the class, perhaps adding a few descriptive notes to help me distinguish among the sea of faces! Real effort is required to learn all the names, but it's definitely worth it in terms of discipline, and you have the added bonus of enhancing the students' opinion of you, since we all prefer being addressed by our name. So for the first few weeks of a new group, spend time each lesson going through the names and make every effort to use names when asking questions and carrying on other types of two-way communication. If you can't remember a name, admit it and ask the student. A few names will stick right from the first lesson, but those of other students will remain hazily in the background unless you really try to master them.

An old technique for keeping order is to 'pick on' students not paying attention and ask them questions. This can be taken too far; students have said to me, 'Why are you asking me, I wasn't doing anything wrong!' Here I was using question and answer

(Q & A) almost exclusively as a disciplinary tool and this was wrong. Students should regard Q & A as a natural part of the learning process; questions should be 'sprayed' around the classroom to keep everyone involved, but particular attention can be paid to students who need to be rehabilitated into the learning process. I return to Q & A in Chapter 3.

WHY DISCIPLINE IS SO IMPORTANT

Discipline is vital for two reasons. First, self-discipline is an essential life skill and is certainly needed in all conventional forms of employment. Second, class discipline is required to facilitate learning. By this I mean that the learning of the majority of the students will be hindered if discipline is inadequate. Discipline can become less rigid and more useful if we realize that it is only a means to an end; we enforce it to enable learning to take place. Therefore absolute silence may not be necessary if students are sufficiently stirred by your teaching to make sensible comments to their neighbours. If you are going to allot more class time for active student involvement, there is bound to be a less highly structured, more free-and-easy atmosphere, with apparently less discipline. However, discipline should still be there; the lesson should still be controlled by the teacher, but there is simply less obvious regimentation. Where some teachers go wrong is to think that 'old fashioned' discipline no longer has a place in modern teaching. You should certainly encourage self-discipline rather than rely on imposing discipline, but while you are introducing less formal, more student-centred teaching methods, don't accept a breakdown of discipline as inevitable. If you have earned your students' respect by being firm and fair from the outset, this will not be in question.

DEALING WITH RUDENESS AND DEFIANCE

I have already referred to how students should address you. Any lack of courtesy to you should be picked up at once. Rudeness and answering back should not be tolerated, but if a confrontation appears to be developing, try to terminate the altercation by politely inviting the student to discuss the matter with you afterwards. You want to avoid providing the rest of the class with a distracting cabaret which they will relish, especially if you come off worse from the verbal exchanges! However, open defiance or swearing at you must be handled firmly there and then: I simply tell the student to get out of my class. What if the student won't leave? If you have made it clear that you mean what you say, he or she will usually leave without demur. If there is open defiance of your repeated request, with other students supporting the miscreant and the situation appears to be getting out of control, this amounts to a classroom emergency.

Classroom Emergencies

Dealing with classroom emergencies puts all teachers on their mettle. This is where experience counts, but a little advice may help you with 'damage limitation'. The golden rule is to remain, or at least appear to remain, calm and in control of the situation. Your aim should be twofold: prevent physical damage to persons or property, and retain your students' respect. So if things are getting out of hand, send a trustworthy student to seek help immediately from a senior member of staff; this is better than going yourself and leaving the class unattended, if at all possible. If a fight has broken out, it's far better to intervene only in the presence of another member of staff, unless serious injuries are being inflicted on a student and immediate attempts to restrain the assailant are imperative. If you are attacked, flight with a minimum of self-defence is best, unless the aggressor is likely to turn on other people. Sometimes students do go beserk; they should be persuaded to leave the classroom and dealt with by a group of staff away from the student gaze. Sometimes irate parents storm into classes; again, try to avoid a confrontation in front of students and call for support from a senior member of staff.

Don't regard yourself as a failure just because you have had some experiences like this and feel you should have handled them better. As teachers, we must be the first to learn from our mistakes, but never dwell on such matters, or you will lose confidence and the enjoyment of teaching. Try to remember that everyone, from the prime minister downwards, mucks things up occasionally; the skilful part is to be able to pick yourself up and carry on afterwards! Even if you didn't need to call for assistance, you would normally expect to speak to the offending student's course tutor or other senior teacher about the matter. It helps to know how the student's other teachers are coping and also if there are any personal circumstances which could help explain his or her behaviour. Sometimes, a pattern will emerge when other teachers are consulted and a collective decision can be made about a student's future. I deal with students who are not prepared to do the necessary coursework in Chapter 4. If you are lucky, you will receive the full backing of your school or college authorities in dealing with student indiscipline.

Sanctions: the Teacher's Legal Position

You should be aware of your institution's attitude towards differ- ent types of sanctions. The more serious ones will be laid down by the local authority or the governing body, but the minor sanctions. will be a matter for the issue of guidelines by the headteacher, principal or director, and subject to interpretation by senior staff. The latter will usually be glad to advise you on the normal practice; you should avoid being put in the position of meting out punishments which are not regarded as 'normal'.

STUDENTS UNDER 18 YEARS OLD

Under English law, a teacher is *in loco parentis* while students under 18 years old are in the classroom, and has the right to take such disciplinary sanctions as a reasonable parent would consider justified in the circumstances. This now excludes any form of corporal punishment for students in state-maintained schools and colleges.

The actual efficacy of any particular sanction must be judged by its ability to help learning continue for the majority of students, and preferably for all. If you ask a student to leave the classroom, you are not helping his or her learning very much, but you may be facilitating learning for the rest of the class, now freed of the disruptive element. However, this brings us to the other side of the coin: a teacher's right to discipline a 'minor' *in loco parentis* is balanced by the duty to take such care as a careful parent would take. Thus, if you put a young child out of class and leave him or her unsupervised, the school could well be held responsible for any accident which befell the child, perhaps by wandering out and crossing a busy road. The law would not expect a similar degree of supervision for a young person of 15 years old. Other sanctions may have legal implications, for instance detentions. All sanc- tions must be reasonable in consideration of the misdemeanour and the age of the student; schools and colleges usually have guidelines.

However much we would like to get rid of certain students, we must always remember two things. First, we are in the business of providing education, not denying it. Second, on a more practical note, there are legal problems in suspending or expelling a student of compulsory school age. Before this position is reached, you should be in discussion with your senior teacher or head-teacher, so that a carefully considered decision can be arrived at after full consultation; the school authorities must be seen to have acted in a fair and constitutional manner. For students above compulsory school age, there is less difficulty, but the authorities still have a duty to act with 'natural justice', which means that a student is entitled to receive warnings (preferably at least one in writing, copy to parents) and to a fair hearing with the right of appeal.

STUDENTS AGED 18 YEARS OLD AND OVER

English law is different for students aged 18 years and over. A teacher is no longer *in loco parentis*, and has no right to apply the types of sanctions appropriate to minors. The relationship between student and school or college becomes a completely voluntary one, with the student being presumed to accept the rules of the institution by his or her attendance. In these circumstances, difficult disciplinary problems have to be dealt with through interviews with senior members of staff, and ultimately by suspension and expulsion. Actually asking a student to leave a course should be rare but not unheard of; it's not so much an admission of failure as a realistic recognition that teaching and learning must conform to certain rules of civilized behaviour like every other organized human activity. However, the rules of natural justice I referred to above still apply, so you must proceed carefully and in full cooperation with senior staff.

The duty of care owed by a teacher to a student over 18 years old is the same as that owed to any other adult. Although parents are no longer legally responsible for their children, most students in their late teens or early twenties are still living at home and financially dependent on their parents, so any contact you can maintain with the parents may be valuable. They can be tremendously helpful in sustaining a young person in his or her studies, provided that a constructive relationship has been preserved with parents during the difficult years of adolescence.

USE OF SANCTIONS

The new teacher needs to appreciate these legal points because they affect the scope of sanctions which can be applied. In general, I am not a great believer in using sanctions regularly; teachers who do are usually those who cannot keep order and maintain respect by the methods I have already recommended. Keep sanctions as a last resort, but don't threaten them without meaning to keep your word. If you have no intention of carrying out a particular sanction, don't mention it. If you spelt out quite clearly where you stood when you first met the class, there is no need to keep uttering threats during every lesson; this simply makes you appear insecure. However, if you do impose a sanction, make sure that:

(a) the culprit, or all of them if more than one, can be clearly identified;
(b) the sanction is appropriate to the misdemeanour, in accordance with the normal practice of the institution;
(c) the course tutor and/or senior staff are informed if the matter is at all serious;
(d) a record is kept of the sanction, and necessary follow-up action is taken, eg to see that extra work set is done.

If you can make sanctions be of a positive nature, so much the better. As in normal learning, doing something constructive is much better than forced inactivity, so try to get miscreants to do something for their punishment that will either help their education or else make some contribution to the community. A little extra homework, if it is relevant and completed quickly, is better than a detention, unless the students use detention time for some socially useful purpose such as tidying up the school premises.

Having said all this, I still feel that the best teachers have little need of formal sanctions; the power to 'fix' a student with your eye and to 'sort out' a student with a few well-chosen remarks after a lesson are worth any amount of formal sanctions. Unfortunately, they only come with experience and confidence in your own ability as a teacher, so be patient and accept your disciplinary mistakes; above all, learn from them!

In most cases, and subject to your legal duty of care for younger children, putting a student out of a class for one lesson is an adequate response to the majority of isolated discipline problems. I've usually found it best to let the matter rest at that; the student returns next lesson and nothing further is said. If the student is gracious enough to apologize, so much the better for him or her, but demands for an apology to mollify your outraged feelings are probably best forgotten, or at least dealt with in a personal interview out of class. There are however a few special circumstances that need consideration in the remainder of this chapter.

Miscellaneous Problems

BAD LANGUAGE AND UNSUITABLE CLOTHING

The use of the odd swearword or obscenity under the breath or accidentally should be ignored. It's best in this day and age for the teacher to turn a deaf ear to such mutterings in classroom or corridor because unfortunately they have become a part of some students' normal vocabulary. However, where bad language is obviously disturbing other students, you must act. I find that a quiet word with the student concerned is the most effective way of stopping it – ask them almost as a personal favour to comply with your request. This also works well if you are faced with a student wearing something outrageous and distracting in class, such as a funny hat. To avoid the possibility of an open refusal to remove the item, which would undermine my authority, I try to approach the student quietly and make a personal request for removal. If the student refuses, you can always have another word after the lesson, but at least you haven't lost face with the rest of the class.

RACIAL ABUSE

There is a disturbing amount of racial abuse that finds its way off the streets into our schools and colleges. As teachers, we must give an example by showing no prejudice of our own and dealing effectively with any manifestations of it in our classes. Students will soon discover whether you are merely paying lip-service to ideas of racial equality. You must be very careful not to make racial jokes or even humourous remarks; if you are teaching immature students, they may take this as evidence that you are prejudiced, and you will have unwittingly confirmed their prejudices. I would try to handle this in a similar way to the swearing problem. If you try to be too heavy-handed with minor or casual remarks, you will only emphasize the problem. If any students deliberately make racialist remarks aimed at discomforting their fellow students, they should be dealt with firmly on the lines suggested above for serious disruptive behaviour. In my opinion, deliberate persistent racial harassment by an older student should result in expulsion.

SEXUAL MOLESTATION

Sexual molestation is something which has come into the news as employees bring cases to industrial tribunals, but it does not seem very common among staff in schools or colleges. However, it is likely that problems will arise where mixed groups of young people gather. Two guidelines should be used here, with a healthy dose of common sense. First, is anyone being subjected to actual physical or mental distress? Second, is the learning process in your subject being adversely affected? If in either case the answer is yes, you need to act, but do so discretely (not in front of the class) and fairly, making sure you have the right culprits. As with fights in the classroom, this is something where discipline is best carried out in consultation with senior colleagues. But do retain a sense of proportion. Don't let every minor incident turn itself into a *cause célèbre*; ignore trifles or you may encourage attention-seekers and those who wish to divert attention from the serious business of learning.

DISRUPTIVE PERSONAL POSSESSIONS

Students sometimes bring items into classrooms which disrupt learning. These may include potentially dangerous weapons such as knives, but items such as personal stereos may cause more distraction in the average class. Your school or college will usually have laid-down policies about what action to take if students do this; consult you colleagues and then adopt a firm line, again avoiding direct confrontation with a student in front of the class. I usually ask the student to put the item right away, not just to leave it on his or her desk to tempt further use. If you have to take the item away, remember that confiscation of something can amount to theft in law unless the item is returned within a reasonable time. For a dangerous weapon refer the matter to a senior member of staff; for something harmless, return it at the end of the lesson or end of the day.

LACK OF RESPECT FROM STUDENTS

Unfortunately, some parents allow their children to cheek them in a way which I find quite distasteful; I don't mean just the playful teasing that goes on in all families, but a real lack of respect. This makes the teacher's job very difficult when dealing with young people, because you must *demand* their respect at the outset and then make sure that you *earn* it as the course progresses. I insist on the use of those unfashionable words, 'please' and 'thank you'. Students must be asked not to sit with their feet up (I used to say to them, 'You wouldn't do that at home', but now I know better!) In fact, in many cases, students must be encouraged to adopt behaviour patterns which they are not used to in the home. Console yourself with the thought that they will need to conform to some extent, anyway, if they are to hold down a conventional job, so the training you are giving them will not be wasted. The paramount idea you need to get across is that whatever standards your students are used to, the ones that will be adopted in your class are *your* standards; stick to them as best you can!

VERY DIFFICULT CLASSES

The more immature and 'difficult' a class is, the more preparation will be needed. My previous remarks on discipline do assume a certain quality of student who is at least amenable to discipline. You may face classes (particularly in your early years of teaching) which we might term as 'beyond redemption'. Here, you forget about idealistic concepts of learning and concentrate on self-survival. You should still try to be as firm as you can, but trying to impose strict discipline without effective sanctions can make you appear ridiculous. To some extent, therefore, you will have to go along with the general way of the class, although you should still refuse to tolerate open defiance. The secret of making some progress with such classes is to keep them occupied. This is where the preparation comes in. You will naturally do all you can to make your lessons interesting and relevant, but you'll have to see that these students are given plenty to do, with exercises, projects, role-plays, visits and so on. This is extraordinarily time-consuming to prepare, but your success with this type of class will be almost directly proportional to the quality of your preparation and your teaching resources.

The majority of 'difficult' classes tend to be in the lower ability range, where the students do not find it easy to concentrate for more than a few minutes. You must accept that learning activities may have to be changed frequently during a lesson in order to keep the students interested and involved. It is true to say that you must become something of an entertainer for these students. There's nothing wrong with this, provided you retain the students' respect and let them laugh with you rather than at you. Often, the students' own imaginative resources may be limited, so you will need more preparation to ensure that students' roles are within their ability, ie they will be able to cope with and get something out of the activities. For instance, a role-play simulation involving an application for a bank loan will only be successful if the students are carefully guided about the sorts of questions asked and the kinds of calculations made in these circumstances.

MIXED ABILITY CLASSES

Mixed ability classes present their own peculiar challenges. With the ending of the old streaming system in many schools, this has become a vital area of teaching. I would suggest that there are limits to the degree of mixing which can occur; beyond them, the effectiveness and efficiency of education suffer. Often, as teachers, we have little control over the mixture of abilities which enter our classes, so we must make the best of it. In any case, you will never find an absolutely uniform level of ability in any class, any more than you will find all the students equally eager to learn! Now there is one technique which is useful here – you can get the more gifted to help the learning of the less able. Group work can be employed in this context; pick your small groups across the ability range and give them tasks which will tax the more able, but leave something for the less gifted to contribute. You must make sure that the latter do not just sit back and expect all the work to be done for them, so circulate among the groups and participate, rather than retreating behind your desk. Try getting one of the more articulate members of each group to report to the class on progress made. The value of these exercises is to get a group of students working as a team – a valuable life-skill in the real world of employment – as well as drawing out the mixed abilities of the group.

UNREALISTIC COURSE AIMS

Problems arise when those in authority mistakenly try to impose unrealistic course aims on classes where some or even all of the students cannot reasonably be expected to achieve them. Being forced to plough through the syllabus of an unsuitable examination is soul-destroying for students and teacher alike. The students will find difficulty in grasping the concept or mastering the skills involved and will become frustrated; learning will be slow; there will be insufficient time for the teacher to use a suitable range and variety of effective learning activities; the students become bored and lose motivation and the result is a wasted educational opportunity. As teachers, we must try to make our representations to our superiors on what is a sound and realistic course aim, given the average level of ability. If these representations fall on deaf ears, we can only do our best for our students, remembering once again that all teaching involves compromise and making the best of the situation we are given. We must try not to let these frustrations lessen our enthusiasm; our aim should always be to do the best we can for our students within the existing constraints, whatever they happen to be.

One compromise solution often adopted for these mixed ability groups is to sponsor the more able for the appropriate examination, leaving the rest to do 'other studies'. I am against such 'sheep and goats' methods, because you get the worst of both worlds. You demotivate the students not sponsored and you make life difficult for the sponsored ones because you cannot give them your full time and attention; it's a form of educational schizophrenia. Now it's quite a different matter to pick out a few of the class to do extra examinations, if they are willing and able, provided the remainder still have the ordinary course examination to aim for. But to leave perhaps half a class believing that they are educational rejects and – what is worse – with no clear aim for the remainder of their course, is both divisive and depressing. The poor teacher faced with such an arrangement can, as before, only make the best of a bad deal, trying to help the more able through their examination and giving the others some relevant activities which may go some way to counteract the demotivation for which the educational authorities are responsible.

TIME WASTED BY INDISCIPLINE

One last point about discipline. The lack of it on everyone's part wastes a lot of time. If you haven't got the self-discipline to prepare properly for lessons, you will waste time fumbling with your notes and materials at the start of the lesson. If your students have no discipline, they will slow down the learning process, or even bring it to a halt. I wonder how many hours are wasted in educational establishments through discipline problems, while teachers try to create some sort of satisfactory environment in which learning can take place? This is why discipline is so important; you must invest time and effort in it when you start to teach, but later it should yield rich dividends in terms of more successful learning.

Chapter 2

Organizing the Classroom and Planning Your Lessons

The longest journey starts with a single step.

Anon

The Classroom Environment

It is difficult to underestimate the importance of the teaching environment. A good environment stimulates interest and motivation, arousing expectations of a worthwhile learning experience; a poor environment depresses and militates against satisfactory learning. Yet this factor is sometimes ignored by teachers who think they are so good that the physical framework of their

39

efforts has little effect on the learning outcome. Educational establishments are not noted for their exciting architecture, and classroom interiors still rely excessively on layouts reflecting the traditional 'students to be lectured at' approach. As teachers, we are frequently presented with unsuitable environments for learning to take place, yet realistically we know that we cannot alter them fundamentally in the short run. Once again, we must make the best of what we have, and here are a few hints for doing just that.

VISUAL DISPLAYS

Quite a lot can be done to improve the learning environment by putting up posters and other visual material on the walls. These can provide a certain atmosphere for a room – one in which the learning process is enhanced. Think of modern theatre – the way in which a minimum of props and scenery are used to suggest a location or a mood. Try to change the material regularly, before it becomes tatty or out of date. As well as providing the right environment, an eye-catching display can provide a focus for a series of lessons, especially of a topical nature.

PHYSICAL CONDITIONS

You should be aware of the main physical things which hinder learning. There are first of all those fundamentals of comfort: warmth, ventilation and light. You will be faced by cold class-rooms on winter mornings; this may necessitate a change of planned activity, with more physical activity and movement between groups in order to prevent rigor mortis setting in among students. Sometimes it is wise to check a room the previous evening or arrange with the caretaker to see that all windows are closed. In rare cases, you may be able to organize a room change, but don't promise this to students before it has been agreed. Don't become drawn into a long argument over whether it is too cold to learn. Some students are glad of any excuse to avoid doing anything constructive, and will spend time sitting in a cold class-room discussing the temperature when their energies could just as well have been channelled into some learning. This really comes back to discipline – you must be positive but fair. Try to take into account all reasonable requests to improve comfort, but remember that you are trying to achieve the best possible learning outcome for the maximum number of students in the prevailing conditions.

The key to your approach should be decisiveness. The classroom is cold, so, right, let's get on with a more stimulating activity this morning. If the ventilation needs adjusting when you enter the classroom, give firm directions for this to be done, and see that your wishes are carried out. Try to get a measure of general agreement for your decision, to make it seem that you are deciding on behalf of the whole group, not just for your own benefit, but be decisive. As leader of the learning process, you should have control over these physical conditions. Your firmness of purpose in achieving your desires in such mundane things, usually dealt with at the start of a lesson, will set the tone for disciplined learning, so don't fudge the issue. Try to ensure that all adjustments to the physical environment are referred to you, so that you have full control, and arguments between students about having windows open or closed are avoided. It's amazing the differences in the clothes students wear; some will have thick clothes, others thin, and you have to keep them all comfortable for learning – a tall order, especially when the thinly clad ones want to sit near the windows and complain when they are opened to satisfy the thickly clad! The worst case is where a hot and bothered student hurries in late and, without reference to anyone, opens the window wide to cool off. You should see this coming, and stop it, suppressing all protest firmly. Actually, the opening of windows to improve ventilation during a lesson is a useful way of providing a short break to bring back students' attention. When in doubt, over-ventilate, because it doesn't take long for a group of students to make a room seem close. Television causes some young people to stay up too late, so you may be faced with students who will only be semi-conscious in your lessons unless you take steps to bring them round.

Strangely, students make much less fuss about light and audibility. Light is one of the primary tools of the trade in the theatre, yet we often ignore its value in teaching. Make sure that each student has adequate light for his or her work, and if you are using a chalkboard, check that reflected light is not making it indecipherable for some students. You can only do this by moving around the room, for students rarely draw this to your attention. Similarly, they will not usually tell you if they can't hear you clearly. Experience will enable you to adjust your voice to suit the size of the room; remember that a loud voice in a small room is very tiring to listen to, so tone it down. Never shout at students to make yourself heard; I have already given this advice. Lastly, be on the look-out for students with sight or hearing handicaps.

Shortsightedness is sometimes left untreated by students anxious to avoid wearing glasses. Insist (not in front of the class) that such students sit at the front, so that they don't pester their colleagues to copy everything on the board from them. For more serious handicaps, you should have had advance notice from the authorities. Make sure that you give such students every assistance. Some of the other students may be rather selfish and intolerant, but you should set an example, bearing in mind that it is now public policy that handicapped students should be integrated with the rest of the community. This can be very demanding, so to avoid allegations of favouritism, you may need to give extra time outside lesson hours to help these students. They are usually well motivated, so the extra effort is worthwhile.

DISTRACTIONS

The more immature the students, the more easily they are distracted, but this affects us all. Why do we find any diversion, inside or outside a room, more interesting than what we should be concentrating on? It's just human nature, and the good teacher accepts this, while at the same time ensuring that lessons are sufficiently gripping to minimize the problem. We can distinguish between two types of distractions: internal and external. You do have some control over the former; some students seem to make it their life's work to stop others learning by forever fiddling around with something. Try not to let them distract you as well, but if they do seriously distract others, you must have a quiet word to make them aware of the adverse effect they are having on the rest of the class. As for external distractions, it's often good to set an example by not letting them disturb you and trying to carry on regardless. A common example is the need to have the classroom door open for ventilation, even if this means allowing in some noise from outside. It's obviously a matter of judgement and compromise, but it's a useful lesson for students to learn that they may have to make a real effort to concentrate on the matter in hand. Don't forget too that your students may be affected by their preceding lesson; learning never occurs in absolute isolation, and you are expecting them to turn their mind to a subject which may need a completely different mental approach from that required in the previous period. Again, anticipation of a lesson following yours may distract them, especially if a test has been threatened! All the time, you will have to strive to maintain attention, using every trick in the teacher's trade to bring this about. A tall order? – yes, but let us call it a challenging opportunity!

Moveable Furniture and Group Work

The greatest environmental problem for teachers is probably that of fixed furniture. I have already mentioned the value for achieving discipline of making sure you can circulate with ease among your students in the classroom, and there's a lot to be said for more adventurous use of class layouts in most rooms. The old-fashioned arrangement, with rows of desks and the teacher imprisoned behind his or her large desk, is quite out of line with modern teaching methods, yet it is surprising how often you see otherwise progressive teachers being content to endure the obvious disadvantages of the traditional layout. If all the desks or tables are screwed to the floor, perhaps you can move the teacher's desk back, so that it does not become such a barrier between you and the class. If the class desks are moveable, you can experiment with half-square or semi-circle layouts, which are particularly useful for discussion lessons. Good quality, stackable furniture is a worthwhile investment in almost any classroom; try to encourage the authorities to spend any money they have on it rather than on gimmicks which will soon be discarded.

REARRANGEMENT OF SEATING
Students are notoriously difficult to move once settled, so try to reach the classroom before they do, and as they arrive, enlist their assistance in rearranging the room. You'll have to allow a few minutes at the end to put things back; once your time is up, you will find it hard to get volunteers to stay after time to help! If you can persuade the authorities to allow desks to remain in the 'half-square' layout suggested above, you will find that it definitely facilitates better learning. The 'back row syndrome' is banished forever, and students will normally be sitting with their backs to the window, so avoiding another potent distraction.

GROUP WORK
Splitting up the class into separate groups, which then get on with their own tasks, is a good way of generating some dynamic tension in a class of students which would otherwise be dull and listless. If you do this, try to arrange the furniture so that students do form proper separate groups. Don't opt out and let the students stay

where they are, unless the furniture is fixed and rearranging it is impossible. Sometimes it is possible for students to turn round and face those behind them in order to make up small groups. Where you can, then, make students move into their groups as a prelude to the work in hand – this gets the lesson started. In order to give students the opportunity of working with different people and also to split up familiar (and sometimes trouble-making) groupings, I ask students to write their names on scraps of paper and then draw 'out of a hat' the members of each group. This in itself generates a little interest at the beginning of a class, which should be sustained by rapidly distributing the work to be done. In effect, by breaking down the conventional groupings of the class, you create some uncertainty, which can then be exploited for learning purposes. This is not very deep psychology, and certainly isn't intended to be underhand, but it does help you to deal with 'difficult' classes which defy all your efforts to help them as an entity.

Teaching classes of mixed ability is a subject on its own, to which I have already referred at the end of Chapter 1. Again, group work can make an important contribution to learning success. From my experience, leaving less able students to learn 'at their own pace' is often a euphemism for letting them fall behind. I prefer to encourage them to involve themselves in group work, where they can benefit from the help of the more able. Does this hold back the latter? I doubt it, except where the exceptionally gifted are mixed with the very backward. What groups can do is to encourage the less able to seek help from their fellows in a more natural way than is possible in the plenary class sessions. Inexperienced teachers often do not realize the extent of their students' reluctance to seek help, not only from the teacher, but even from fellow students. In the context of group work, asking questions and helping each other becomes a natural part of the learning process. It can even be argued that the more able students benefit by having to internalize and then express in their own words and demonstrate the ideas and skills they have successfully absorbed.

Group work is of course even more useful for better motivated and more mature classes. Here, you can stimulate useful discussion of the topic in hand, moving about the classroom to provide encouragement and help. Don't hover around the same students for too long or you will inhibit them, but resist also the temptation to retire to your desk and get on with some marking while the groups begin to lose interest and start discussing. last night's television programmes. I return to class discussion in Chapter 3, but I want to emphasize here how important classroom organization is in facilitating learning by these methods. When the group work has ended, wherever possible some form of plenary session should be held, so that students will gain the benefit of other groups' thoughts. Try to persuade the spokesperson for each group to come to the front and address the whole class. This makes more of a spectacle, and helps to prevent the other members of the group distracting the speaker.

SEATING ARRANGEMENTS FOR ROLE PLAY

The effective use of role-play is also dependent on an appropriate classroom layout. This useful method of getting students to act out various roles for learning purposes will be considered in Chapter 3, but in order to ensure some chance of success you must arrange the furniture so that there is an open space where the role players can perform and be seen and heard by the rest of the students. Again, don't let the players remain in their seats; prise them out, because you will achieve a much better effect if they come forward and perform at the front. Bring some simple props: a hat, scarf or sunglasses can make the role-play more fun; don't forget that students can learn especially well when they are enjoying themselves!

Timetables, Class Composition and Class Size

Three other factors impinge on classroom organization: timetables, class composition and class size.

TIMETABLES

Effective use of class time is at the heart of my thesis, and the timetable rules this. Be aware of the relative merits of different times of the day for learning purposes, and try to set your programme accordingly. The earliest lesson of the day may not be a good time to have an activity, such as a test, which you want all students to undertake, if you know that some are almost bound to come in late. The last lesson may be equally unsuitable for anything demanding too much concentration. So take advantage of times when students are (relatively) fresh to stimulate their intellects with new topics, and liven up end-of-day sessions with group work. Try to plan at least a few lessons ahead, so that the learning activities are in harmony with the time of day and the state of your students.

For the individual lesson there are certain factors you should bear in mind. We can identify three segments of the typical lesson. First, there is the 'settling down and getting going' time, when students' thoughts and activities need to be directed towards the learning process; this is often punctuated by late arrivals. Second, there is the 'core' time, when the most effective learning is likely to take place. Third, there is what I call the 'looking at watches' time, when concentration starts to wane and the students need further stimulation to maintain their learning until the lesson's end. We should consider more carefully the so-called 'fatigue factor' in learning. Research has shown that in any time period you may be able to improve performance by training and practice, but there will come a point within that time period when fatigue starts to set in and performance begins to suffer. The skilled teacher will be able to sense when that time has arrived: there will be signs of restlessness, students' eyes glaze over, performance of the task in hand will slow down and mistakes will increase. This is the time to alter the tempo of the lesson by a change of activity, indeed you should plan your lessons to anticipate these moments with changes in learning activities. I cover the pacing of lessons in the next chapter.

CLASS COMPOSITION

Class composition may well be beyond your control; a new teacher is usually allocated a class and must make the best of it. Beware of drawing hasty conclusions about the class as a whole and particularly about individual students within it. Be optimistic about their learning potential until you have firm evidence to the contrary, subject to establishing a firm disciplinary regime from the outset. Nevertheless, you should be aware of the basis on which the students have been assembled. In many schools and colleges, systems of streaming and setting are still used. *Streaming* attempts to put together students of similar ability, so that learning can take place most effectively. Some experts have suggested that streaming tends to reflect parents' socio-economic classes rather than students' ability or potential. *Setting* tries to get round this by dividing students up according to their ability in individual subjects. The trouble with these arrangements is the well-documented effect of bringing about a self-fulfilling prophecy, or 'give a dog a bad name'. Students do tend to behave in the way they are expected to, so putting a student in a low stream or set will usually ensure that he or she conforms to that standard, regardless of whether a better standard could be achieved. There is some evidence that mixed ability classes compensate for this 'negative labelling', but at the expense of making greater demands upon the teacher; I have already referred to this in Chapter 1. Many of the strategies for student-centred learning I suggest in the next chapter will have to be pressed into service whatever way your classes are composed; the chances are that, as a new teacher, you will be given the lower ability students into your charge, so don't concern yourself too much about streaming and setting – accept what you are given and see if you can make learning take place!

CLASS SIZE

Class size is something else over which teachers often have very little control. There's no doubt that a large class is usually more difficult to handle in disciplinary terms, and you may have problems in rearranging large classes for effective group work. Generally, the recommendations I have made for dealing with difficult classes apply even more where they are of large size. You have more problems of audibility, visibility and access to students at their desks. It is therefore even more vital to maintain firm control by the methods I have suggested, and wherever possible split the class up so that smaller scale learning and interaction between groups of students is encouraged. The great temptation when faced with a large group is to lecture them. If they are well behaved, they may accept this without demur, and you may be lulled into believing that a lot of learning is taking place; usually it isn't. If the students are not well behaved you will soon find your lesson deteriorating into chaos. In either event, you must adopt some student-centred learning strategies to ensure that some learning does take place. On the other hand, if you are faced with a very small class, perhaps fewer than six, it is difficult to have group work, but of course the opportunity for more individualized teaching is valuable compensation; you can ensure, indeed you must ensure, that each student makes a worthwhile contribution to every lesson.

OPTIMIZING THE LEARNING ENVIRONMENT

Your whole purpose should be to make maximum effective use of the room available for learning purposes, just as the producer of a play tries to make the most out of the stage area. Try to mould the physical environment to fit your teaching strategies, rather than vice versa; but if you can't change things, at least be aware of the constraints and adapt intelligently.

Outside Visits

Don't forget that you are not always restricted to the classroom; outside visits should be a feature of many courses, even though they do need careful organization. The key points are all pretty obvious, but, as newspaper 'horror' stories show, are sometimes overlooked:

(a) Apply for formal permission from the school or college authorities for the visit. You may need to consult the local authority also.

(b) Obtain the written consent of parents of all students under 18 years old for the visit, unless it involves going somewhere within walking distance for less than a full day.

(c) Make sure that any money needed is collected in advance and properly accounted for.

(d) Ensure that there is an adequate staff-student ratio for the age of student being taken, with at least one teacher or other responsible person of each sex for a mixed class going on a visit of more than a few hours.

(e) For students under 18 years old, you will be *in loco parentis* for the entire visit, so take care not to neglect your charges, arming yourself with a full list of names, home addresses and telephone numbers. Make sure that all students are returned to the pre-arranged termination point.

(f) If you are using private cars to transport students, make sure that the motor insurance covers such 'business' use.

(g) Check that your school or college has proper accident insurance to cover outside visits; this is usually automatic if you have followed all the laid-down procedures, but don't take this for granted; always make sure you are adequately covered before you go.

(Incidentally, it's worth making yourself familiar with all the insurance arrangements in your school or college; various schemes are in operation, but it's an area that is all too often ignored by teachers.)

In all the hustle over making the arrangements, don't overlook the learning value of the visit. Brief your students beforehand on its significance and the things to look out for. You may wish to prepare a worksheet to be completed during the visit, or to be used in class afterwards. Alternatively, the visit could form the foundation, or a component, of a project. A set of questions could be prepared in advance to form the basis of a class discussion after the visit. Whatever you do, make sure your students extract the maximum learning benefit from a visit by carefully priming them beforehand and making it clear that afterwards they will have to use the knowledge gained in class activities.

Use of Teaching Aids

I now consider the various teaching aids which can help you implement your teaching strategies. The main choices are handouts, worksheets or workcards, textbooks, overhead projectors, slide projectors, audio, video, computers and boardwork.

HANDOUTS

Preparing handouts costs time and money, but they do save time in class as against writing an exercise on the board. I use handouts for sets of figures or diagrams which need to be reproduced pretty exactly. If you don't label the handouts too specifically for a particular class, you will be surprised how often they can be used for other classes, provided you keep a copy with your teaching notes to remind you of their existence. (I say this because it's very easy in the first few hectic years of teaching to forget what you have prepared, and end up redoing handouts unnecessarily.) Be careful to avoid a 'guilt complex' over handouts: some teachers feel that they must provide a handout for virtually every lesson, almost to compensate in some way for inadequate teaching. Use handouts to supplement your students' learning, not replace it.

WORKSHEETS OR WORKCARDS

You will also need to produce handouts if you rely on worksheets or workcards for some of your lessons. For some subjects, there is now a variety of these available commercially, yet experience shows that on many occasions you can get better results by using your own creations. Why is this? Mainly, it is because you can tailor your worksheets to suit your students. Of necessity, commercial productions have to be suitable for a wide variety of students and courses, and it is rare to find a set of worksheets that fit in exactly with your needs. Sometimes this drawback is outweighed by two factors: the saving in time by obtaining ready-made material and the professional finish which makes the worksheets look more attractive. Alternatively, use extracts from newspapers and magazines; these often contain material not available elsewhere and are generally presented in an interesting way. (Obtain advice about copyright if you are uncertain of the legal position.) You can add some questions underneath the extract for an exercise or discussion session.

The actual use of any kind of worksheets has been questioned recently. They are regarded merely as a method of keeping students quiet; words such as 'mindless' are applied to them, implying that there is no real participation by students in any meaningful learning. Well, I have found worksheets useful, provided they are not abused and over-used. By all means devote a lesson, or better still, part of a lesson, to doing worksheets, but don't expect your students to endure lesson after lesson of them. Also, make the sheets themselves stimulating; if they are too hard, most students will give up trying, and if they are too easy, they will complete them too quickly and possibly regard them as an insult to their intelligence. This is why it is vital to fix the right level of difficulty. Other points that may help are to consider group work on worksheets rather than always making them a solitary activity, and to use the sheets to assess progress by taking them in at the end of the lesson for a quick perusal. In these ways, you can make worksheets into a valuable teaching tool.

TEXTBOOKS

Textbooks are a traditional teaching aid, but they should not be dismissed just for that reason. On the contrary, a good textbook can facilitate more student-centred learning by releasing the teacher from having to impart large quantities of information by traditional lectures and note-giving; instead, students can undertake supervised self-tuition and the time saved can be used for activities which reinforce and assess learning. There are plenty of textbooks for most subjects, but ones which suit *your* teaching style are not so easy to find. Recommendations by more experienced colleagues will help, but you must use a textbook which you can get on with, and this can only be found out by trial and error. Make use of publishers' inspection copy services where available; don't be afraid to send books back if they are obviously unsuitable. Before sending for a book, ask if any of your colleagues have a copy tucked away somewhere; they may be able to lend you a copy and give you an opinion on it into the bargain.

If you can find a suitable textbook, use it sensibly as a foundation for study; it can often provide a basis for your course programme (to which I shall return later in this chapter) and for homework (dealt with in Chapter 4). A relevant, well-presented, up-to-date and stimulating textbook is worth its weight in gold, provided you use it as a means of enriching your students' learning rather than an excuse for skimping on your preparation.

To get the most out of textbooks, you should be aware of their drawbacks, and act accordingly. There is the problem of inflexibility. How often have we seen quite a good exercise in a textbook, only to find that its angle of approach or the subject matter covered do not coincide fully with our own, so that the students would be more confused than helped by doing it. Furthermore, if students have their own textbooks, there is a strong possibility that at least one student will forget to bring the book, even if you remind them the previous lesson; and sometimes you will not realize you need the books until part-way through the lesson (even with that forward planning I advocate!). You can make a general rule that the main textbook should be brought to all lessons, but this works only if you do use them regularly; students will soon not bother to bring books if they are not used. If the authorities can run to the cost of a class set of books, all well and good; it does wonders for your muscles carting them backwards and forwards! Beware of undue dependence on textbooks. If you become a slave to a book, your spontaneity will be dulled, and your students may decide that your presence and their attendance are superfluous. No textbook can generate the same enthusiasm as a vital human being can, so don't abrogate your responsibilities; you should be more than a mere interpreter of a textbook.

OVERHEAD PROJECTORS

Much is made of overhead projectors (OHPs) in teacher training colleges, and they definitely have their uses, but again don't rely too heavily on them. They do have the advantage that material, especially diagrams, can be drawn accurately in advance, thus saving lesson time. Use of transparency overlays can be very effective, although coloured chalks can do a similar job. With OHPs, you avoid the problem of having your back to your students, as you do when using a chalkboard; this is most valuable if discipline is a problem. It is worth developing your OHP technique by familiarity and practice; the visual impact of silhouetted shapes as well as drawings and words can assist learning considerably. Try to set up and test your OHP before the lesson (this advice applies of course to all types of equipment). If you can arrange to have an OHP permanently in the classroom, so much the better, because there is more danger of the bulbs blowing if OHPs are moved when they are warm. Even the latest models make quite a disturbing hum, so they should be turned off as soon as they have served their purpose. Also, not every classroom has a suitable screen or light-coloured surface for showing OHPs. Finally, it's easy to get so wrapped up in your marvellous OHP transparencies that you lose the rapport and immediacy of your classroom presence – you become an OHP operator rather than a teacher. This applies to all types of teaching aids: don't use too many at once, and make sure they don't take over your central role of seeing that learning is taking place. One day in the not-too-distant future we may have display panels linked to computers, so that the teacher can provide a large visual display of any text or diagram; until that day comes – and even when it does – we must make sensible and selective use of the technology available.

SLIDE PROJECTORS
Slide projectors must not be forgotten as a teaching aid. Well-chosen illustrations bring a subject to life, and the cost of commercially produced slides is within the budget of most institutions. You may be able to take your own slides, or at least you can produce your own sequences by loading them into a carousel and afterwards storing them in a special wallet.

FILM AND VIDEO
Film is still a valuable source of audiovisual material, but the wider availability of video has led to a revolution in the audiovisual departments of schools and colleges. Students are used to watching television at home, so you don't usually have much difficulty in persuading them to allow the video to roll; whether any learning takes place is a different matter. If a video is to have any learning potential, you need to persuade your students to extract something from it. More able classes should be asked to take notes on the main points, to form the basis of a discussion afterwards, or during the next lesson. Less able classes should be told that they will be questioned or given some sort of group work afterwards, perhaps a project, or you can even arrange a quiz with teams. Only in an emergency should a video be used as a 'fill-in'; try to integrate videos into your course programme and follow

them up with appropriate student activities.

The following are a few practical tips for using videos. Even though they are pretty foolproof, do try the machine out and locate the part of the tape you want before the class starts, if at all possible. Remember that glare on the screen from windows may spoil some students' view. Check on the running time; you can always fill up a lesson after a video finishes, but it's not so easy to break off three-quarters through one. If you can, choose videos which last for no more than half the lesson; then you will have time for a discussion or related activity while the video is still fresh in your students' minds. Otherwise, follow up with the activity in the very next lesson, or through some homework. Consider using clips from videos lasting no more than two or three minutes to illustrate your teaching; this is far better than succumbing to the temptation of using videos as 'lesson fillers'.

AUDIOTAPES

Audiotapes should not be overlooked as a teaching aid. There are many excellent educational radio programmes which deserve a wider audience. They are very suitable for more able students, who have a longer attention span and can concentrate on the spoken word. Even so, you should integrate these tapes into your lessons in the same way as videos; I often help my students by writing key points on the board while the tape is in progress, so that proper notes can be taken by them. Records and now compact discs are also valuable for these purposes; teachers of music and drama will not need reminding of their utility.

COMPUTER-ASSISTED LEARNING

Computerized aids to learning are being hailed as the answer to all the teacher's prayers. Remember that they are only a more sophisticated form of teaching aid that will not replace the teacher. What they can offer is interactive learning, that is, the machines – for that is what they are – can respond to students' learning needs in a flexible manner which facilitates students' active participation. Software is gradually being introduced for all kinds of subjects, but my caution about commercially produced worksheets applies equally here: make sure it suits your students and fits in with their course programme; don't let the computer tail wag the learning dog. Before you get swept away with enthusiasm for computer-assisted learning, consider whether it is the best way for helping your students learn; as with any form of teaching aid, it can become an end in itself rather than the means to that end.

Various computer networks are now being created, such as TTNS and Prestel in the UK. These offer the keen teacher and student a veritable mine of information and almost infinite possibilities to harness these exciting developments in the cause of successful learning. As teachers, we shouldn't be left behind, so make sure you are up with your students, who will have become familiar with computers from an early age. Keyboarding, word-processing and spreadsheet courses are available, so find out what INSET (in service training) courses you might take advantage of. It's no longer possible to leave computers to experts; every teacher should be 'keyboard conscious', so if you believe in equipping yourself for the future (and not just your students), make sure you keep up with the new technology – it won't go away!

BOARDWORK

You will find that many experienced teachers rely heavily on boardwork. (This usually means the chalkboard, but the whiteboard is now used increasingly as well, since it has no dust problem.) Teachers still find that the chalkboard offers many advantages in terms of immediacy, flexibility and reliability. Ideas can be gathered from a class and quickly displayed for all to see. Diagrams can be altered with the flick of a duster. Provided that you have suitable chalk (I always carry a supply in a small polythene bag in my pocket) and a handy duster, the only technical problem that may arise is if the board surface is difficult to write on and reflected light makes visibility bad for some students.

So what is 'good boardwork'? Writing legibly on a board comes with practice, and so does the ability to reproduce diagrams accurately, even for those of us with no artistic ability. Scruffy boardwork is usually a sign of poor teaching, because it can confuse. Treat the board as the collective notice board for your class; nearly everything that goes up on it should be part of the mainstream of your lesson. If you have to make a digression, for instance to answer a student's particular point, mark off a corner of the board and use that. Don't mix up main points and sidelines so that the board becomes a confused mass of notes and jottings, because your students' notes are likely to reflect this. Make clear when you are gathering ideas and putting them on the board that you will be drawing up a more systematic list in a minute. I often draw a line down the centre of the board and put ideas gathered from the class on one side, and then rearrange them with additional material on the other side, so that notes can be taken in an ordered form.

You will have to accept that a diagram or set of points cannot appear by pressing a button as is possible with an OHP, so there is a time factor to consider. In fact, you will be surprised at how fast you can become in putting things up on a board. There is still, however, the drawback of having your back to the class. If possible, go into the classroom early and get some of your boardwork done in advance. If not, your disciplinary ploys should have ensured that mayhem does not break out when you turn you back, but it's still unsatisfactory to lose a lot of eye contact with your students. So turn round and look at your class frequently when you're involved in boardwork. We're all told not to talk to the board when teaching, but it's awfully difficult not to do this. Try to get into the habit of turning sideways as you speak, so that you can refer to the board while addressing the class. This needs a conscious effort, but otherwise you will become like an orchestral conductor – more familiar from the back view. One other point: it's good professional practice to leave the board clean when you vacate the classroom; you need to earn your teaching colleagues' respect as well as that of your students!

USE OF ILLUSTRATIONS AND DIAGRAMS

Students remember more that they see than what they hear, so words actually presented visually on board or OHP do have greater impact than mere oral tuition. But pictures and diagrams connected to these words are even better, so wherever possible try to illustrate your lessons. Much of what we teach in any subject is concerned with classifications and relationships: the connections between things. Try to develop a repertoire of simple diagrams which will add a little interest and visual effect to your presentations. The simplest diagram can be like this:

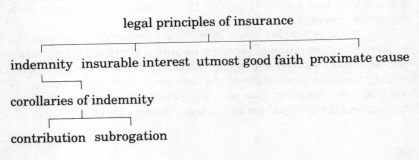

legal principles of insurance

indemnity   insurable interest   utmost good faith   proximate cause

corollaries of indemnity

contribution   subrogation

This could act as the introductory diagram to a series of lessons. Although contribution and subrogation will be dealt with as separate topics, I want to convey the fact that they depend on the main principle of indemnity. I could have listed the principles 1 to 4 and called contribution and subrogation 1(a) and 1(b), but I think a diagram gives more impact here.

Likewise:

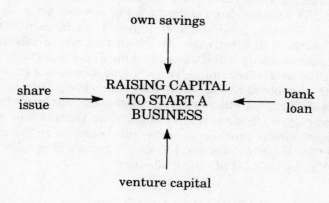

You can go round each 'spoke' of the wheel and explain more. Sometimes it's best to present the whole diagram to start with, so that students can appreciate the overall picture at once. On other occasions, you will gain more attention and anticipation if you build up the diagram a bit at a time. This also avoids awkward gaps while you are waiting for the slower students to copy a complete diagram.

One more example: while teaching economics, you wish to explain the interaction of people's unlimited wants and the world's limited resources, which brings about scarcity and thus forces society to make choices about the allocation of those resources. A very simple diagram like the one opposite can help fix these fundamental relationships in students' consciousness:

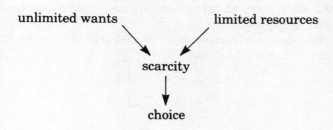

If you start a lesson with a diagram, it helps to settle the class, because they will usually begin to copy it from habit, and so attention is gained. It can then provide the focus of, and the structure for, the remainder of the lesson. Alternatively, a diagram is a good way of providing a slight change of activity; if students have been concentrating on listening to you, or doing a written exercise, the act of assembling the necessary drawing material and producing the diagram provides a small release of tension which helps to recharge their batteries of concentration. Remember also that diagrams help to break up your students' notes and make them easier to revise from.

Try not to introduce diagrams right near the end of a lesson if this will mean you won't be able to finish using them. Not only will you have the extra work of putting the diagram up again next time, but also some of its impact will have been lost. Trying to rush through a diagram at the end of a lesson when students' concentration is waning will not achieve satisfactory learning. It's better to use up the last few minutes of the lesson with a spur-of-the-moment exercise (more about these in the next chapter), and save your diagram for an effective start next time.

You can of course save time by providing a handout of a diagram but you'll find it hard to explain without having a board or OHP diagram to refer to, and the students will be looking at their copies instead of at you. Usually, it's better to involve your students directly by getting them to draw diagrams themselves; they should be actively involved at all stages in the learning process. Again, go round and check their work – if two lines have to intersect at a particular point, you're sure to find someone who has drawn up a new set of scientific rules so that they don't! Waiting for the slowest students to make a work of art of their diagrams is a waste of time; they can always take them down in rough form and then work them up into a masterpiece in their own time (but check that they do).

Symbolic diagrams can act as a sort of shorthand. I use a stylized drawing of a factory like this:

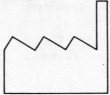

to represent production for business studies classes. It's surprising the number of combinations in which you can use this type of symbol. Any type of visual representation beyond the most obvious can usefully be employed to make an impact on your lessons. Think of the presentations you have attended which you can recall easily; wasn't there some visual item which stuck in your mind, perhaps seized your imagination? There probably was, so do recognize the vital contribution that sight makes to learning. We can build our lessons around a diagram or picture, using it as the centre-piece of our presentation. Many successful lessons do this, just as the careful placing of a relevant and eye-catching picture or diagram in a magazine or newspaper article helps to provide a focus for the text.

USE OF ACTUAL ITEMS AS 'PROPS'

Your diagrams and pictures form part of your 'props', adding another dimension by supplementing words. But why not add a third dimension to your lessons? Use actual items as exhibits. This is standard practice in science and technical subjects, but how often in other subjects do we talk about things without making any effort to reinforce our teaching with exhibits placed there on our desks. Obviously, this can be taken to ridiculous extremes, but it's surprising how often we can use physical objects to explain abstract concepts. For example, we conventionally use the choice between oranges and apples when explaining the economic theory of consumer choice. You may disagree, but to have an apple and an orange actually on my desk, handling them as I explain, seems a valuable aid to stir interest and help remembrance.

APPROPRIATE USE OF TEACHING AIDS

Two final points about teaching aids in general. First, experience will enable you to achieve the right 'mix' of them to emphasize both sight and sound, and the optimum number of aids for any one lesson. Second, don't let your lessons degenerate into a series of 'effects' like a theatre performance; always question the appropriateness of an aid, and employ it only if it improves the chances of learning taking place.

Syllabuses, Course Programmes, Lesson Preparation

SYLLABUSES

Teachers often feel constrained by syllabuses – the need to 'cover' (whatever that means) a certain body of knowledge and collection of skills in a certain degree of detail and to a certain level of competence. Yet I would argue that teachers do not discharge their responsibility to their students simply by covering the syllabus; this is a secondary aim. First and foremost they should try to generate interest and enthusiasm for the subject in its own right; from this will arise the motivation for the student to participate profitably in learning activities. Of course, the competent teacher will monitor very carefully the class's progress through the course programme which may be based on a syllabus, but if too much emphasis goes on 'syllabus teaching', the result for many students will be disappointing. Students will not have had any enthusiasm generated – they will fail to see the relevance of the subject and refuse to take it on board as part of their equipment for life. They will try to 'learn' a subject simply to pass an examination and even on this criterion their success is likely to be limited if their enthusiasm has not been aroused.

I do not wish to denigrate the value of the syllabus. It does provide discipline for the learning process, indicating the areas of knowledge and skills which are considered relevant. Frequently, the teacher needs this discipline, because otherwise he or she succumbs to the temptation to follow every byway and even blind alley which presents itself during the course. No; learning has to take place within certain constraints, like every other human activity, so treat a syllabus as a challenge rather than a strait-jacket, and be grateful that it does give you some idea of what learning outcomes are expected.

How can we apply these ideas in practice? First, recognize that your limited resources – time, energy, materials, photocopying and the like – will restrict your ability to achieve your goals. So we must use the available resources wisely. Of these, time is the most valuable. Effective teachers don't waste time moaning to their colleagues about all the things that need to be done; they get on with them. I'll return to time management in Chapter 4, but let's consider how you can best use your time for preparation.

Course Programmes

Every course of education and training is something like a journey you are starting on from here, the first class and, we hope, is going somewhere. So you and your students need a map. Copies of this vital document – course programme, scheme of work, call it what you will – should be distributed to your students during the first class, not promised for some vague future date. This means that you must have done your homework checking course aims and regulations as laid down by senior staff, examination board syllabuses and other official bodies. If your main aim is an examination, your course programme should conform fairly closely to the syllabus. Remember, however, that a syllabus is not meant to be a course programme, so you must design your own. Syllabuses tend to be rather vague and obscure documents, so you will be doing your students a service if you can interpret what is required and assemble it in a meaningful order. Often, you will not wish to teach the subject in the same order as the syllabus, so use a pencil and eraser to juggle around with the various parts until you achieve a reasonable compromise. Textbook contents pages are useful here, since they show you how experienced teachers and writers have tackled syllabuses.

The main object is to make your course programme into a working document, which both you and your students can refer to during the course. Try to produce a plan for active learning, that is, a programme of what students will be doing in order to learn. It may be helpful to produce your plan as a flowchart or critical path diagram, emphasizing your critical learning objectives. The more vocational and skill-orientated the course, the more activity-based should be the programme. Inevitably, academic subjects will have a course programme which is more knowledge-based, but some indication of learning activities such as projects, surveys and role-plays should be given along with the areas of knowledge to be tackled. Programmes are usually a compromise, because you must take into account the constraints of hours available, the need for integration with other courses and the logic of the subject. If you can use the holiday breaks as natural divisions between the various main portions of the programme, so much the better. I like to set the programme out in numbered weeks and also put the actual date of the week – eg Week 2 beginning Monday 9 September 19–. If there is space, you can also put in details of recommended reading, course regulations and any examinations; you will usually need to give advice about these matters at the first class.

Finally, do try to have a reasonably professional job done of typing and photocopying the programmes. I used to type them with my old portable on to banda masters and then present my classes with insipid-looking documents. Then I used a word processor and a modern photocopier and students actually commented on how much more interesting the course looked – on paper, that is! As teachers, we ought to take more care in our presentation and marketing. We blame lack of time, yet a small investment of time in the packaging of our courses pays rich dividends.

Making course programmes available to all your students has several advantages. As an enthusiastic teacher, you should have prepared the programme anyway, so the only drawback is the cost of reproducing copies for all. This however is a small cost to pay for giving your students a valuable study aid and showing them that you mean business, giving the impression that the course has been carefully prepared and you know exactly what you are about. This again will help discipline and set a good example – if you aren't ready for the first class, how can your students be expected to adopt a serious, committed attitude when it comes to handing in work on time?

Lesson Preparation

Lesson preparation: what pleasant hours we whiled away at training college producing lesson plans and beautiful OHP transparencies! How soon we came to realize that the real teaching world leaves little time for such niceties, except when we are being assessed by our seniors! Some teachers just give up trying and, having 'mastered' their subject, simply fall into a rut of oral tuition for generations of students to endure. In effect, they are teaching their subject, but not their students. We mustn't give up; we are trying to equip our students for life.

We should therefore adopt a business-like approach to the learning process, being aware of our objectives, the ways of reaching those objectives, and the methods by which we can check on progress – assessment – while the process is continuing. The trouble with some lessons (and after all most courses are mainly a series of lessons) is that students are not made aware of the lesson's context. Education and training are made available in penny parcels, so that the broader structure of the course and its ultimate aims are lost in a welter of detail. Now a criticism of some of the newer, less traditional courses is that they adopt a 'broad brush' approach, and seem to be a little light on detail; the more erudite knowledge and skills are filtered out, leaving a course which appears to be a mere shadow of its former self. While there is a grain of truth in this, we must remember that the aims of courses are changing; people are recognizing the fact that in order to equip our students for life, we need to offer them a broader education than previously. Of course, 'broader' tends to imply 'shallower'; I think that we are still trying to reach the stage where we can properly identify and teach what our students really need for their life equipment. In the meantime, the new teacher must to a large extent be guided by his or her more experienced colleagues. Do study syllabuses and other material so that you have the best possible appreciation of what the course you are teaching aims to achieve. Usually, the implementation is left very much in the hands of the individual teachers, so you are put on your mettle to design a programme of activities which will deliver the course in the most effective way.

Before every class, try to spend a moment considering what contribution to this equipping for life is going to arise from your teaching – or rather from your students' learning. If you can't think of anything, then quite simply you are wasting your students' time, not to mention your own. Many syllabuses are now being expressed in terms of behavioural objectives – what the student is expected to be able to do at the end of the course. Unfortunately, these objectives are often couched in vague terms such as 'be aware of' – a favourite term which means very little to me. However, you can use these objectives as a basis to visualize what your students should be able to do with the knowledge and skills you propose to cover in the next class. The teaching of skills is usually easier in this connection, to the extent that you can assess progress more readily. For teachers of knowledge, it is much harder to come up with satisfactory ways of assessing progress, yet this assessment is a key to effective teaching, and I shall return to it in Chapter 4.

You need an aim for each lesson – not necessarily very detailed, but at least something that is sufficiently clear to enable you to express it to the students – because they should be made aware of the purpose of each and every lesson. The seeming obsession of teacher trainers with lesson plans is for the very good reason that you should have considered both the aims of your lesson and its implementation *before* you go into the classroom! Now, as you become more experienced, you will be able to do this quickly and almost intuitively, but to begin with you ought to give lesson planning the time it deserves. Even experienced teachers need to put their lesson aims across to their students, and they must plan to have the materials they need available for a particular lesson.

When you are planning lessons, try to consider carefully the practicalities of your plans. With experience, you will become able to estimate fairly accurately how much time each different learning activity will take, so that your lessons will run closer to your plan. To begin with you should build in enough leeway to ensure that lessons can be kept on an even keel. To continue the nautical analogy, use your lesson plan as a navigator uses a chart – so that he knows what is ahead. The teacher is always expected to know what should happen next in the lesson, because he or she is in effect the 'captain' of the learning vessel. If you lose your way during a lesson, it can be very disconcerting for your students, so make sure you are prepared before you set sail. This is not to say that your lessons should be devoid of surprises; they help to raise interest and give variety, but they should not be unexpected to you as well – incorporate them into your plan to add a little spice to your lessons. It's sometimes nice to shoot the rapids, so long as you are confident of not ending up on the rocks!

Chapter 3

Achieving Student-centred Learning

We hear, we forget; we see, we remember; we do, we understand.
A more authentic old Chinese proverb.

Learning and the Use of Concepts

What is learning? Is it the same as understanding? – These questions have exercised minds more clever than mine, but I would suggest that we can proceed in steps. To start, let us consider conditioning. A stimulus leads to a simple response, as when you withdraw your hand from touching a hot surface. Much of a child's early learning is based on this process, which forms the foundation of the more advanced forms of learning, the aim of which is to bring about either a change in our students' behaviour or a change in their knowledge, or usually both.

ACTIVE UNDERSTANDING

The higher levels of learning involve active understanding, ie the ability to apply something learnt to a slightly different set of circumstances. We must distinguish here between passive and active understanding; our students may experience a sudden flash of perception as described in Gestalt psychology, but may still be unable to apply what they have grasped – this is passive understanding. Active understanding comes when our students can apply their learning and see it in relation to other concepts. Indeed, learning involves our students in the constant absorption of little skills and concepts so that, having mastered the simple, they can concentrate their energies on the more complex. In these ways, learning passes from the teacher to the students – teaching has brought about learning!

USE OF CONCEPTS

Most learning uses concepts. We cannot proceed very far in communication without conceptualizing our thoughts. In Chapter 2, I used a diagram to show how in economics we start from the simple concepts of unlimited wants and limited resources to arrive at the slightly more complex concepts of scarcity and choice. We can then build on these foundations a body of increasingly sophisticated concepts, which, taken together, form the subject of economics. We can indeed speak of first order concepts, second order, and so on. In mathematics, distance is a first order concept, while speed, being distance divided by time, is a more complicated concept of the second order. What is crucial is that we appreciate what level of concept we are using, and make sure that we introduce concepts to our students in the right order.

Nearly all knowledge-based teaching, and a good deal of skills teaching, depends crucially on the teacher being able to make his or her students understand concepts. There has been much criticism of the use of rote learning in this context; this is misguided to the extent that every student must learn some things, such as the alphabet, by heart. Rote learning should be employed to facilitate understanding and application, which we may regard as the true objects of our endeavours. Indeed, there is plenty of evidence that memory and recall are greatly assisted by understanding. I never understood chemistry at school, and failed miserably when I attempted to learn chemical equations by heart instead of trying to appreciate the underlying concepts.

Experience has shown that there are a number of techniques

which help in the teaching of concepts. Always start from the simple and the familiar, and move to the complex and the unfamiliar. The simple concept will usually be the one your students have already understood, so you can build on that foundation. While you are moving to the complex, resist the temptation to bring in distracting material, for example, exceptions to a general rule. Focus on the pure concept you wish your students to understand; the time for elaboration is after the concept itself has been grasped. Many students have difficulty in coming to grips with concepts in an abstract way: they need concrete examples from the real, tangible world to make the ideas come alive for them. Try to take these examples from students' own experiences; again, be careful to avoid very distracting examples, but any attempt to relate a concept to your students will be worthwhile. Once the concept has been understood on its own, you can then show how it fits into the wider context of your subject, and deal with corollaries, exceptions and other points related to the central concept.

Positive Reinforcement of Learning

Your students' learning can be enhanced by encouraging every step that they make in the direction of understanding. This goes back to conditioning; we reward a correct response to a stimulus, and thus make it more likely that the response will be correct next time. The most effective reward is one that tells students at once that their response is right, and encourages them to proceed further. Even if their response is incorrect, they should be made aware of this in such a way that they will try again to get it right. In educational jargon we say that 'immediate positive feedback' helps learning. You must try to provide plenty of what is called 'positive reinforcement' to your students, encouraging their progress by rewarding them. If you tell a student off for the incorrect response to your question, that negative reinforcement may make him or her remember that the response was wrong, but it won't do much to assist the learning of the right answer, and it will probably make the student reluctant to offer future contributions.

I referred to rewarding students in order to provide positive reinforcement. This is a tricky thing to do in practice. Educational experts recommend that lower ability groups need more tangible rewards to encourage their learning, although as teachers we are not usually in a position to offer material inducements such as sweets. More intelligent students are satisfied, it is said, with 'symbolic' rewards, such as being told, 'Well done!' Teachers have to rely heavily on the symbolic variety; it can be quite effective, if given sincerely and coupled with the use of the student's name. What you must avoid is congratulating all students equally for their contributions, because then students will not realize when you are trying to reward them particularly. Be selective: show your gratitude for all contributions, but reserve special praise for those which represent a real step forward in the learning process. Experience will help you appreciate what constitutes a meaningful reward for different students; some need a lot of verbal encouragement, others are eager to please you, and help themselves with only an occasional word of acknowledgement.

Student-centred Learning

Once we realize the importance of giving positive reinforcement to our students' learning efforts, the next step is to enquire into the best framework or context for those efforts; in other words *how* will the learning actually take place? The proponents of the 'discovery' and 'active' learning methods advocate very similar objectives: helping students to learn by discovering for themselves in what have been described as 'doing situations'; in effect, learning becomes for the student something active rather than passive. What is the justification for these methods? There is none better than that which forms my quotation at the beginning of this chapter: it is by *doing* that we understand; but let us see why this is likely to be so.

How do we learn most of our everyday knowledge and skills? Why, by trial and error, learning from our mistakes. Now, if this is a natural way of learning in the real world, should we not adapt the method for classroom learning? Educationalists sometimes refer to 'experiential learning' to emphasize the element of experience and involvement that is entailed. Both 'doing' and 'being taught' are experiences, but the former must bring about greater understanding: it must be more relevant to students than passive listening. Instead of students merely letting lessons wash over them, they can be rewarded in a positive way for agreeing to become actively involved in the learning process. What is more, there is greater scope for treating students as individuals, since each student has the opportunity of applying his or her individual ability to the learning activities. At the same time, cooperation between students can be encouraged, according to the activity chosen; students can help each other learn, they have the experience of teamwork (needed for many jobs) and class morale and identity can be enhanced. I prefer to use the term 'student-centred learning' to cover all these similar approaches, because it focuses on what the student is doing rather than the teacher's antics.

ORAL TEACHING

I suppose the majority of teaching is still done by word of mouth in *telling* our students something and expecting them somehow to grasp our vocalized thoughts and make them their own – 'internalize' them as the jargon goes. Time and again I have seen what many would call 'good teaching' going on, yet there is little evidence of effective learning. We still cling to our oral tradition, perhaps reaching back to the Middle Ages when most people's idea of learning was listening to a sermon in church. The trouble with oral teaching is that from a learning point of view it is so passive – the most we expect our students to do is to take notes, answer a few questions and stay awake! This is where student-centred learning scores: it brings out the best in teachers. Like an elephant, a good teacher is difficult to define, although you will probably know one if you see one. Good teachers vary their approach according to their students and a host of other factors, but you will always find that their methods are student-centred. Now the hard-pressed teacher will say, 'Yes, agreed, but *how*, in practical terms, can I apply this philosophy in the classroom?' The consideration of this question will take up the rest of the chapter.

PROBLEMS OF STUDENT-CENTRED LEARNING

Let me say at once that compromise is necessary. You soon realize that only a percentage of your lessons will be first-rate learning experiences for your students. If you reach 50 per cent, I reckon you are doing very well. Why is this? Well, partly it is because education and training are very inexact sciences. This is one of the hardest lessons for any new teacher to learn – and believe me, we learn far more than our students in our early years of teaching! Partly also, we should appreciate the inherent problems of student-centred learning. One of these is that it may demand more resources than traditional methods: extra time is often required for lesson preparation and a larger amount of physical equipment may be needed. Another snag is that if it is not handled with a sure touch, it can be a recipe for chaos in the classroom. What is more, with some subjects, such as chemistry, there is some inherent danger: students must not be expected to discover the explosive properties of potassium through unsupervised experiments! Lastly, there is a minority of students who benefit more from a very structured approach to learning and are inhibited by unfamiliar learning methods. To this argument I would reply that nearly all British and American children get used to student-centred learning in primary school, and some students' reluctance to become involved in this method of learning later on is more due to poor motivation than any natural dislike of the method used.

TEACHER COMMITMENT

Despite the high level of commitment that a student-centred approach demands of the teacher, there is usually no problem, because the new teacher has the enthusiasm, if not the experience, to make a success of the method. Placing our students where they should be – at the centre of the learning process – requires a real effort for most of us, but it must be made, because this is where the greatest dividends can be reaped in educational terms. In its broadest sense, education is equipping our students for life; we would consider it strange indeed if we equipped our young army recruits by giving them a gun, a manual, and some lectures!

PACING OF LESSONS

Implementation of student-centred learning brings out the difference between the experienced and inexperienced teacher. For example, the correct pacing of lessons is vital. Some lessons drag and become boring to the students simply because they are taken too slowly. Teaching textbooks recommend a 'brisk' pace, and this is probably the best word to sum up what your approach should be: forward-looking, positive and creating eager anticipation, rather than hesitant, apologetic, languorous and plodding. You set the tone of the lesson as soon as you walk in – that is why the start is so important; having begun with some bounce, you create momentum to help carry you through the lesson. Whatever activities you have planned, see that the pace is not allowed to flag. It's best to err on the fast side, being mindful of the fact that some students may be left behind. If you can keep moving so that the majority are learning satisfactorily, you will have more time to come back and help the minority you lost on the way. The nature of the subject may constrain you; if the topic is one which is a foundation for further study, you must be satisfied that all have understood. Even so, beware of putting too much faith in a verbal explanation. If, say, half the class has understood a point, it may be more productive to get them all doing an exercise; I return to the value of exercises in Chapter 4.

STUDENT EXPLANATION

You should encourage students who have grasped a point or mastered a skill to explain it in their own words to their fellow students. Never be afraid to allow time for this; the learning potential of such situations is often underestimated. No teacher should be so arrogant as to believe that he or she is always the best teaching medium! Some students may have gained an insight in a way not realized by you, which can then be passed on to others, and students may in any case be more willing to listen to the explanations of their fellows. Also, the very act of explaining a point or demonstrating a skill helps to strengthen their own understanding and competence, giving them a certain pride in being able not only to master something, but also in being able to pass it on to others. Remember, some of those you teach may be the teachers of tomorrow, and some of them will have a greater talent for teaching than you!

CIRCULATE TO CHECK UNDERSTANDING

Now it's all very well encouraging this sort of method, but we must keep the momentum going, making sure that students don't waste the available time by idle chat. So you should circulate rapidly in the class, listening to the conversations and helping where required. This will help you to check if any incorrect learning is taking place; there is always the danger that a student who has 'got the wrong end of the stick' will compound his or her error by misleading someone else. Try to nip these problems in the bud, but don't forget that teaching is an inexact science, and that you will probably get a better overall rate of effectiveness by brief explanations and class exercises, rather than by long-winded oral repetition; remember – ' . . . we do, we understand'. If you find that a minority of students still haven't grasped the essentials of your lesson, you can either devise fresh exercises for the next lesson, or arrange to see the students separately: if the topic is not central to the course, you can simply note that it should be given more attention when revising.

Class Discussion

Sometimes, class discussion is used by teachers to cover up for lack of lesson preparation, but it can be an effective teaching method. The key is to distinguish between chatting and discussion. The latter has an aim or purpose which the teacher should have settled in advance. So if you are going to discuss the fairness of the electoral system, you should have a list of points that should be covered, and see that these are brought out. It will help if you have been able to ask your class to read up on the topic, and students being human (yes!) it's better to get them to write down the main points they have discovered so that you can check that the preparation has been done. Alternatively, you can give them an extract from a newspaper, journal or book to study for a few minutes at the start of the lesson. These methods provide a basis and stimulus for discussion. While it may be easy to start a discussion over a drink in a pub, it's not so easy in the artificial atmosphere of a classroom, so you will find it easier if you have something with which to get things started. An audiotape or video can serve the same purpose, but if it lasts for a whole lesson you'll have to get students to make notes as they go along, so that they will remember enough for the subsequent discussion.

INVOLVE THE WHOLE CLASS

For a discussion to be effective, you must involve everyone, and see that they take something away in written form as a permanent record. Involving all students is essential, otherwise the keener and more articulate ones (usually sitting near the front) will make all the running, while the rest of the class discusses last night's television programmes or looks out of the window. Here, the physical configuration of the classroom is vital. If at all possible, arrange the seats so that no one has his or her back to anyone else, so all discussion can take place face-to-face. Please refer to Chapter 2 and the sections on moveable furniture and group work.

RECORD POINTS AND ENCOURAGE STUDENTS' OWN IDEAS

The need for achieving a permanent record of discussions should be assisted by the teacher unless the students are mature enough to take all their own notes unprompted. The main points which emerge can be put up on to the board, usually after some 'processing' by you to transform them into a logical set of points. How is this done? You are trying to draw on students' knowledge and opinions (sometimes no more than prejudices) to obtain some generally accepted wisdom. Be careful not to try to impose your own modes of thought on your students; it's vital to get them to articulate their own thoughts – this is a 'doing activity', and much more valuable educationally than any amount of spouting on your part. Of course, you want them to appreciate the accepted wisdom which they may have to master for examination requirements, but educationalists – and examiners – increasingly recognize the importance of learning being *internalized*: taken over as his or her own by each individual student, used by them on their own terms, and given that unique individual slant which we call character. So don't stop students expressing ideas in their own way, and try to use their own words as far as possible when putting up a summary on the board. Don't force your students into a fixed mould; as a preacher once said, 'We all come out of the same mould, but some are mouldier than others!'

Coping with Wrong or Extremist Contributions

Some students may offer erroneous views. Don't allow them to be ridiculed by other members of the class, or they'll never contribute again. Show your gratitude for their contribution, pointing out as diplomatically as possible their error, and trying to guide them towards the truth. If a student tries to use your class as a vehicle for his or her extremist views, don't be afraid to make your disagreement plain, and try to deal rationally with the arguments put forward. However, such bigots are not easily converted, so if you don't want the rest of the discussion taken over by them, you should use your authority as discussion leader to courteously but firmly put the lid on it, if necessary offering the student the opportunity of pursuing the matter further after the lesson; only the most fanatical will avail themselves of this opportunity.

Encourage Reluctant or Introverted Students

What about students who will not say anything unless prompted? You must try to get them involved; if only 8 of the students contribute out of a class of 24, two-thirds of the class will not have participated *actively* in the learning process. It's a fascinating trait of human character that causes some people to be extrovert and willing to air their thoughts in public, but which leaves the introverts naturally reticent. Try to ease the introverts into the discussion by asking them questions which you are pretty sure they can answer, and not just by 'yes' or 'no'. Don't pick on any one student for a lengthy series of questions, but 'spray' your questions right round the class. You may have to restrain the more extrovert in order to give the quieter ones a chance, but always do this with courtesy, trying to keep the momentum of the discussion going. A complete mastery of your students' names is essential, so that you can turn rapidly from one to another.

SUMMARIZE THE DISCUSSION

When all the planned points have been covered, or time is pressing, round off the discussion with a short verbal summary, the main points of which should be on the board and in your students' notes. An effective discussion will have enabled all students to have wrestled verbally with at least some of the points covered, and therefore will have at least partly achieved the aim of student-centred learning.

THE QUESTION AND ANSWER METHOD

I return to question and answer (Q & A), because it has been an important teaching technique since the time of Socrates. Its usefulness is manifold: encouraging participation, revealing understanding (or lack of it), and even for discipline – to arrest the attention of errant students. As with all useful teaching devices, there are pitfalls. It can waste a lot of time if you try to elicit replies which are obviously unobtainable, either through ignorance or – much worse – because you worded the question badly. Try to frame the question properly before you ask it; you shouldn't need to add bits to explain it. Thus: 'Karen, what is positive economics? . . . I mean, how does it differ from normative economics? . . . Well, what is the difference between a positive and a normative statement in economics?' By the third attempt, the teacher is getting at what he really meant to ask. He realizes that the first question is too abstract for a concise, one sentence answer, and then starts groping towards what he really wants to ask. This wastes time and flusters Karen, who gives up on hearing the first question. If you ask too many questions which your students cannot answer, you will just turn them off. Try to set the level of your questions so that at least some of the class can answer, but regularly adjust the level downwards so that the less able have a share of correct answers, and don't forget to praise all genuine efforts to answer. Failure to answer a question is a negative learning activity; success acts as a positive reinforcement of something learnt. So use Q & A to build up students' confidence in their own knowledge, rather than to display their ignorance.

You should make your students get used to a regular amount of classroom interaction; they should come into your class prepared to converse intelligently, accepting this as part of the educational process. For many students, this will need great encouragement from you. Research has indicated that 80 per cent of responses from students to teachers' questions are in the form of a one syllable answer. The solution is to frame your questions so that they elicit longer replies. Think of a game of tennis between a coach and a learner; the coach returns the ball to the learner so that he or she can have further stroke practice, rather than smashing the ball out of play to show off the coach's superiority. Likewise, we must resist the temptation to display our erudition at our students' expense; we can earn our students' respect without going to those lengths.

Q & A is essentially an exercise in two-way communication, which once again will only be fully successful if the whole class is involved. It takes a real effort to ensure that *all* students do their fair share of answering. Often, the keenest students are also the most articulate, sitting at the front and supplying ready answers to all your questions. (Note that the most articulate students are not necessarily the most able in your subject; quiet students may lurk at the back of the class, and need 'bringing out' by your judicious use of questioning.) You can easily be misled into thinking that the performance of the keen few reflects the progress of the entire class. In effect, you are judging the class by its best, or at least its most articulate students, and turning a blind eye to all the shortcomings which are no doubt dormant in the back rows. Don't repress the keen students too much; let them have their say, but avoid conducting a trio or quartet when you are supposed to have a full orchestra in front of you! To ensure full participation, address most questions to named students, not to the class in general. Start with the student's name, then put the question briefly and concisely. If you pick on someone after the question, you may have to repeat it because the student wasn't listening, and one of the keen students may chip in before you do pick on someone. Lazy students will try to avoid making any effort by saying that they don't know the answer; if you think that they can be helped to find the answer, persevere, giving hints and encouragement, while keeping the keener ones (who may be bursting to supply the answer) quiet. It's a matter of judgement to decide when you have spent as long as you can afford on one student in this way; they may become embarrassed if you try to force their mental processes too far. Often, class neighbours will whisper the answer to the student you have picked on; when the latter suddenly perks up, make it clear that you know where the answer came from and then ask the same student another question, so that students will appreciate that cribbing from another is not an easy option to satisfy you. A minority of questions can be addressed to the whole class, where you just want to find out if anyone knows about a particular matter, but most Q & A should be done on a named basis. It's a simple and effective way of encouraging students to think and internalize knowledge, because they must express it in their own words.

ORAL COMMUNICATION

At the start of this book I was rather scathing about the oral tradition in teaching. We do tend to judge a good teacher by his or her ability to communicate orally, although I would contend that much more than this is needed for learning to take place, in accordance with my ideas about student-centred learning. Nevertheless, our ability to use language as a method of communication is the main thing that separates us from animals, so we shouldn't dismiss this gift of nature too easily. The good teacher uses language as a kind of tapestry on which to embroider his or her ideas; communication between teacher and students is therefore still vital even if we now place the students' learning rather than the teacher's teaching, as our centrepiece. So, how is effective oral communication achieved? If our students simply *note* our communications, either in their brains or on paper, this is not truly effective communication, because surely there should be some *understanding* of the message. To check on this, we must actively involve our students. So you see that a student-centred approach can help to reinforce oral communication, rather than replace it.

THE 'HIDDEN CURRICULUM'

The trend is now towards the common core curriculum, but we must not let this blind us to the fact that children and young people learn much more about life outside the formal curriculum than they do within it. We can divide the 'hidden curriculum' into two parts: the part learnt at school and college through the values and messages put across by teachers, and the part learnt at home, in the street and in clubs from any one with whom the students come into contact. The classroom learning situation is a very restrictive and artificial one, but it has to make up for some of the deficiencies of the other learning environments. You will be aware that many teachers are worried about the lack of conversation at home, sometimes caused by antagonism between the generations, sometimes the result of laziness by parents, and probably most often the outcome of too much television. There is also concern about negative attitudes to the learning process which may be picked up in the home and through the general social environment. I have already mentioned the resultant difficulty many young people have in handling abstract concepts which form the basis of much of our communication.

BRIDGING THE COMMUNICATIONS GAP

There's no doubt that some people are born better communicators than others, because personality has a part to play. However, most of us have to make an effort to 'tune into' our students' wavelength. This doesn't mean introducing all the latest fashionable words into our teaching, but rather ensuring that our sentences are not too long and complex, and that our vocabulary is within their grasp. Well-educated teachers are apt to forget that some young people can only command an extremely limited vocabulary. Mildly technical terms which you are perfectly at ease with may cause no end of problems – the word 'deficit' is one which has troubled my business studies students on many occasions – so watch out for expressions of puzzlement on the faces of your students and be ready to offer patient explanations of any difficult word, trying to give some concrete examples as illustrations. We have to come to terms with the communications gap that inevitably exists between us and many of our students. To bridge it, so that we don't talk over their heads, we also have to avoid talking down to them, and we must not fall into the trap of trying to become 'one of them'. We need to make a conscious effort to communicate effectively by choosing simple words and phrases, and involving our students through student-centred techniques so that they can become comfortable with language. Then we can attempt to get on to their wavelength by relating to their own life experiences in our teaching, while at the same time trying to widen their use of language and enrich their appreciation of the experiences life has to offer.

ORAL INTRODUCTION TO A LESSON

Nearly all lessons begin with some talk, which sets the scene for the planned learning activities. If you are teaching some knowledge or skill today, you may well have to rely on the time-honoured ploy of 'talking through' what you are about to demonstrate. This is really a form of oral introduction to the lesson's learning activities: the language precedes the illustration by boardwork, demonstration and student activity. Be careful to give your 'talking through' impact by gaining the students' attention and keeping it. Students can get used to ignoring teachers' introductory remarks, because they are addressed to no-one in particular and are regarded rather like the overture at an opera – the accompaniment to the audience's settling down. You can take steps to avoid this by using Q & A right from the start to command attention. Make your opening remarks brief and concise; sometimes the teacher is not tuned in sufficiently quickly to the class, so spends the first five or ten minutes searching audibly for the right approach. This may be accompanied by lots of 'ums' and 'ers', the students gradually losing what interest they did have until the teacher suddenly comes to his or her senses and says, 'Right, now let's start work!' Now if you do not want to be a slow starter like this, you must see that you have your ideas focused before you enter the class. Sometimes you can't do this because you have rushed from one class to another, so take time after you make your entrance to collect your thoughts before starting; it's far better to use time like this rather than to launch into some incoherent burble to which no attention is paid. Alternatively, give yourself some breathing space by getting the students to start some kind of activity while you are sorting yourself out – something referring back to the last lesson, for instance.

Have you ever listened to a recording of yourself giving a lesson? You may find that you speak in a series of incoherent phrases which do not form logical sentences, linked by those 'ums' and 'ers' I referred to above. Try to make every word count in class; inexperienced teachers think that they must fill every silence with a torrent of words. Don't fall into this trap; command attention, speak concisely, and shut up. The oral part of lessons can be used to introduce a topic, yes, but its main purpose must be to enable students to internalize what you are trying to teach them; in effect, we want our students to teach themselves. If we can help them with their own oral skills, we shall not only be facilitating learning on their present course, but also providing them with a vital life skill which may be of more value than almost anything else we can offer.

Written Work and Notes in Class

Turning from oral to written work in class, brings me to the matter of note-taking for knowledge-based subjects. It is still the case that much of the examination system is based on testing knowledge retention and reproduction. You would think in these days of photocopying machines that people would no longer set such store on students being able to reproduce their notes from memory. Thankfully, the emphasis is changing to the testing of more valuable real-life skills involving knowing where to find knowledge and how to apply it, but even so, the ability to retain knowledge is still pretty important for many courses.

Students of more tender years have funny ideas about their notes. They almost invariably expect the teacher to provide a full set of notes which will enable them (if only they learnt them) to be able to tackle any examination question. For a start, I hope that we as teachers would say there is more to education – any education – than simply passing examinations. Apart from that, we would like to think that the transmitting of knowledge is more than a purely mechanical process; it should promote some *response* on the part of our students. For these reasons, I do feel that we should try to get away from dictated notes, copied notes and handout notes wherever possible. I say wherever possible because I recognize that there are circumstances where it is appropriate to use these methods, but we shouldn't rely on them to the exclusion of what are recognized to be educationally superior ways of achieving the same result.

Students expect notes – they complain bitterly of teachers who 'didn't give us enough notes'. Probably the teacher gave sufficient actual information, but did not ensure that it was recorded by the students. Note-taking is a form of discipline and therefore you must start as you mean to carry on. Like class discipline, you will find it harder if your students have already got into bad habits. Try to get them to take their own notes. It's very difficult to teach this and besides it may not really be your job. Like a roadsweeper's job, it's the sort of thing your students will have to pick up as they go along. Before you start an explanation, say that you will expect them to make their own notes at the end. If they wish, they can jot down the main points in their rough notebook as you proceed. During your explanation, write any unfamiliar terms on the board and you can even put the main points up to give students a structure or set of 'pegs' on which they can hang their notes. Having done your part, ask your students to write up their own notes. Once again, go round the class – it's amazing how the teacher's approach can galvanize students into putting pen to paper! See that most students have made satisfactory notes; if there is time, give on-the-spot help to any students who are stuck, otherwise see them afterwards. The secret of this technique is to avoid wastage of time at the start and end of the note-taking sessions: at the start, students may gaze around aimlessly until spurred into action by you; at the end, they may lapse into time-wasting chat unless you cut short the session and forge ahead. There will always be a few slowcoaches who will have to finish later, but check that they do complete their notes. Parkinson's Law will apply if you don't make clear that time available for note-taking is strictly limited. A series of sessions of explanation and note-taking helps to break up the lesson, giving students a better opportunity to internalize the knowledge offered and givingyou the chance to check on what parts of it they do not understand.

Check Students' Understanding of Texts

It's surprising how reluctant even some of the more mature and responsible students are to sit down and do serious reading and note-taking in their own time. A good way of ensuring that they do read, absorb and produce a permanent record, is to set questions on each of the main points, in the same order as the text. The questions should try to extract the essence of the arguments, but avoid the possibility of answering by mere copying, the object always being to ensure a true understanding of the text. I find this a useful way of encouraging my students to do background reading in the holidays. You can ask for the answers to be handed in, and it doesn't take long to skim through them just to check on reasonable compliance with your wishes. Of course, preparing the questions as a handout takes time, but there is no easy way to make sure that your students really do undertake their background reading.

Value of Study Skills

There are many good study skills guides on the market, and serious students should be encouraged to invest in one. Some institutions set aside time at the beginning of their courses for an introduction to study skills, including note-taking, the use of libraries and catalogues, and the following up of references. This is time well spent, because it encourages those students who want to get the most from their studies, but lack the confidence and know-how to proceed independently.

WHEN TO USE DICTATED NOTES OR HANDOUTS

When is what I call 'spoon-feeding' unavoidable? First, when you are short of time and feel that the need for speed outweighs the educational drawbacks of dictated notes. At its simplest, this could be near the end of a lesson – perhaps an interruption beyond your control has put you behind and you feel it would be inappropriate or wasteful to have to explain a point a second time next lesson, so you decide to dictate your own notes direct to the students. You may be behind with your course programme through no fault of your own; there may have been a timetable change reducing your class contact hours or some other administrative cause, or even your own illness. If you are seriously behind – say by more than five hours – you must decide whether to carry on at your previous pace and simply omit some part of the course programme, although not necessarily the last part. If this is done, be sure you inform your students and explain to them what is happening; get them to revise their copies of the programme. Alternatively, you can decide to gain time by issuing handouts on a topic that is suitable for this treatment, so that some class contact time is 'saved'. You can still assess learning by setting a class exercise after students have read and prepared the topic as a homework. If you like, you can make the homework the actual obtaining of the topic material, provided that:

(a) material is readily available;
(b) you specify exactly what is required (there might be a safety problem if you were vague about the collection of poisonous mushrooms, say);
(c) it is structured in a way that fits in with your course programme;
(d) you can check that students actually complete the work; and
(e) you still do a class exercise to assess learning.

What you mustn't do is panic when you fall behind schedule and try to rush through the course. Trying rapidly to 'touch on' topics, or 'run over them briefly' (they are indeed usually flattened afterwards), is normally counter-productive because students become confused and unsettled and are made to feel insecure from what they perceive to be a lack of professional expertise on your part.

The second justification for spoon-feeding is when complicated technical knowledge must be communicated in a precise form. A legal or scientific definition needs to be absolutely correct, so you must write it on the board or dictate it word for word. Diagrams for engineering or economics cannot be imagined by students out of a vacuum – they must be copied from the board or a textbook. Even copying has some educational merit – it involves doing something and possibly provides scope for setting exercises to see if students have any understanding of what the diagram is trying to express. Handouts can help where something is quite complicated and its actual construction is not relevant to the course. For example, if your students are studying the structure of local government, it will help them to consult a map showing how the country is divided up into local authorities, but it is not necessary for them to have to draw the map. You could however get them to write in the names of local authorities and list their functions as a class exercise. Again, you may wish to discuss a particular theme in general terms, perhaps a facet of government policy, but need to provide your students with adequate background material, such as a chronological list of all relevant legislation and government decisions. Make sure you give students time (and the motivation) to study your handouts, preferably by making them the basis of homework and a class exercise. Keep copies of handouts for absent students, putting their names on the top so that you know who needs a copy next lesson. You'll also need to keep a few copies to lend to students who may forget to bring their own copy to the next lesson when it is needed. Try to encourage students to see that all your handouts have a purpose, and require a response from them. If your handouts are like your teaching – disappearing into students' folders without having any noticeable effect on the students themselves, then I'm afraid your technique needs an overhaul!

Team Teaching

There is an increasing emphasis on the *integration* of learning, that is, the setting of subjects in a wider context and showing how different subjects are interrelated, as they are in the real world. All individual teachers need to be aware of the wider horizons of their subjects, but it is often felt that the delivery of a truly integrated course needs a pooling of talents in the form of team teaching.

The mere formation of a team does not work a magic spell to

produce an integrated course. Poor teamwork may lead to worse results than the dedicated labours of one individual. If you are put into a team, or have to organize one, there are certain cardinal points to watch. It should go without saying that meticulous planning is essential to ensure that all student activities conform to an overall, integrated plan. This should enable all members of the team to know their place in the overall scheme of things throughout the course.

As a team member, you must act professionally and pull your weight, that is, contribute adequately. This really touches on your relations with your colleagues, to which I return in Chapter 5. Team teaching really does test your ability to get along with other teachers, because you have to modify your pet teaching methods to fit in with other people's ideas for the good (we hope) of the students. So this really does involve some give-and-take; teams of teachers who are incompatible on a personal basis rarely work well for very long. The best teams are built on the foundation of each member's respect for the talents which the other members can bring to the team. If we are supposed to try to recognize the potential for progress in our students, how much more should we respect our colleagues' efforts, even if we may sometimes believe they are misguided.

Good communication between team members is vital. Students will soon become dissatisfied if they experience conflicting instructions, overlap of teaching and a generally disjointed delivery of their course. Formal team meetings should be timetabled on a frequent and regular basis, but there is a limit to what can be achieved at these. More valuable are the brief discussions between team members which may be needed on an almost daily basis. These enable minor difficulties to be sorted out before they become major problems. Try to keep in constant touch with your team members, and never begrudge a few minutes' consultation at any time. Quite simply, the better the communication between team members, the better the chance of producing a truly integrated course.

Student Activities for Better Learning

In the last part of this chapter, I shall consider the contribution that various kinds of student activities can make to better learning. (The use of exercises for learning and assessment purposes is covered in Chapter 4.)

ROLE-PLAY

Role-play is one activity that has not been exploited to its full potential by most teachers, probably because it does require some thoughtful preparation. There are however quite a few packages now available on the market; some can be readily adapted for general class use. Not every student likes to act out a role, and getting volunteers is never easy, but there are usually a few people willing to cooperate. You can always involve the whole class by splitting it up into groups and giving each group the task of producing a short play to be acted out by all the group members. One or two absorbing and amusing role-plays by a keen group of students is worth a lot of chalk and talk. Treat role-play as a normal learning method: it is really just an extension of the 'learning by doing' philosophy. We teach a skill by making our students practise it themselves; if we can persuade them to learn knowledge through applying it in the context of situations approximating to the real world, surely this can only help our efforts, bearing in mind the communication problems we have already considered. So do take full advantage of this student-centred method, using it to bring variety and a breath of fresh air into your lessons. Don't forget to arrange the classroom for maximum effectiveness, as suggested in Chapter 2. You won't usually need to spend a whole lesson on a role-play – just a few minutes may suffice, perhaps as the centrepiece of a lesson. The thoughtful preparation I mentioned earlier will entail working out a scenario and the characters involved, but need not include actual dialogue, which should be made up by the role players. Really, it's not as difficult as it sounds, and is usually popular with the students if you give them plenty of guidance and encouragement, and provided that you don't overdo its use; regard it as one of a variety of teaching strategies at your command.

CASE STUDIES

Case studies can be used in a similar way to role-plays, because you can involve your students in reacting to a situation expressed in written form. The main problem is obtaining suitable material and making it available to the students. Many textbooks now incorporate case studies in their exercises. Newspapers and periodicals offer many up-to-date and relevant articles that can form the basis for work which can grip you students' interest, if you can provide thought-provoking questions to answer on it. In some subjects, examination boards are turning to case studies for testing purposes, and old exam papers are a good source of material. Various educational bodies connected with industry are willing to provide material; this is invariably well presented, but you need to be selective in choosing the right level and content for your students. In many cases, material which has been heavily edited and predigested loses its impact, which is why I often prefer raw, untreated items from the current media; these tend to reflect more of life's complexities and ambiguities, which is no bad thing for teaching purposes – sometimes we over-simplify the real world so much that our lessons lose all verisimilitude. So make a real effort to collect every type of media communication that can form the basis for a case study: newspaper and magazine cuttings, radio and television programmes, and extracts from books. Copyright and producing sufficient copies of written material are the two major difficulties which need time, persistence and resources to overcome, but even if you only read out a passage from a book, it may have an arresting effect on your audience.

DATA RESPONSE QUESTIONS
Data response questions are an extension of case studies, and make use of suitably presented information on which students have to answer questions by interpreting the data. The best exercises use genuine data from reputable sources and ask searching questions which help students to understand its significance. Again, exam papers are a good source of material, and many government publications are a mine of stimulating information.

SURVEYS AND QUESTIONNAIRES
It is even better if we can help our students to collect their own data for analysis. Surveys and questionnaires are ideal ways of achieving student involvement and generating interest in the subject matter. You will have to put in some preparatory work on the design of the survey, but your students may be able to draw up the questionnaire. As with all student-centred learning, don't rely too much on any one method of delivery, so avoid endless surveys which become mere routine. Initiate a few good ones on relevant topics, and leave your students to do most of the donkey-work under your supervision.

PROJECTS
Another favourite device for student work is the individual, group

or class project. Now, since projects have become so fashionable in education circles, they have tended to be abused as a learning strategy. If you can avoid the pitfalls, projects can be an absorbing activity for students. Group or class projects must ensure that everyone has a specific and preferably identifiable contribution to make, otherwise some students will 'freewheel'. Working together in groups does encourage the valuable skill of cooperation, but as we have seen, you must keep an eye on what is happening in each group. Trouble arises if the absence of one or more group members prevents the others continuing with the work, or if a member of the group lets the others down by not doing the task allotted, for instance obtaining some information. There is also the problem of marking accurately the contribution of each student if the project forms part of an overall course assessment.

If you arrange individual projects, don't make them too large, especially for less mature and/or less able students; they will not be able to cope with planning to complete something in six months' time. Either split the project up into smaller, more manageable sections, or, better still, have a series of less ambitious projects on different topics to keep up interest by novelty. Always offer plenty of advice on how your students should go about doing their project, or their energies may be channelled in the wrong directions. If possible, help them plan their project in advance; the experience of doing this successfully will be at least as valuable as anything they will learn from the project itself. Choose project topics which are not too vague and all-embracing: 'The Countryside' would be too broad for most students, but 'Wild Flowers' or 'Farm Machinery' would provide a better focus for their efforts.

The key to successful project learning is for the teacher to monitor the students' work regularly and frequently. Perhaps a lesson can be set aside periodically for this purpose; you will need to get together with each individual or group, sorting out and resolving all the (sometimes infuriating) reasons why students have been unable to make progress. Try to keep calm and help your students to see that it is a valuable skill to be able to plan and produce something to a set timetable; they will appreciate your assistance later in the outside world.

BOARD GAMES

The use of board games is frowned upon in some quarters, yet so many good ones have been introduced recently that you would be unwise to dismiss them as frivolous. They have been used to train industrial managers for many years, and are particularly useful for giving practice in decision-making. In fact, any sort of game may have a place in your teaching strategies; there are types available for nearly every subject, from farming to stock exchange speculation. Research has shown that young children learn a great deal from playing games, and we can capitalize on this by either using existing games or designing our own. I include here quizzes, crosswords and every other type of challenging activity which can provide variety to a course. Games are a good way of involving those students who are naturally diffident and retiring in more formal classroom situations; inhibitions are lost, or at least forgotten, while a game is in progress. It is nearly always worthwhile to encourage student participation through games, and we mustn't forget that they can help us cope with those 'awkward' classes and 'difficult' times of day when learning – any learning – is an achievement!

OVERALL AIM OF STUDENT-CENTRED LEARNING

It's very easy to get so involved with the day-to-day concerns of trying to produce effective learning experiences for our students, that we tend to forget about our primary purpose: equipping our students for life. Children and young people should be able to select certain parts of the curriculum to make especially their own; to fasten on to some areas of knowledge and skills which appeal to them, so that they can develop strong foundations on which to build their future careers. We should always be on the look-out for these developments, encouraging our students to experiment and taste all areas of the curriculum, so that they can find their own niche. The longer I continue in this profession, the more I realize that the key to successful teaching is to concentrate on your students' learning by getting them to do the work; don't 'overteach': arrange everything so that they are involved in the learning process up to the hilt.

All too often, students leave full-time education with no idea about what they want to do with their lives, because they have found nothing which stimulates their interest at school or college. As teachers, do we not have a responsibility here? In our teaching, we should surely remember that when we try to deliver a curriculum by means of learning experiences and activities, we are trying to bring out the innate abilities of our students, for their own benefit and that of the community. This is a rather altruistic idea, I know, but sometimes in the midst of our teaching we need to ask ourselves what our vocation amounts to, and how we can use student-centred learning to equip our students for life.

Chapter 4

Assessing Progress and Coping with the Paperwork

Education is what survives when what has been learnt has been forgotten.
B F Skinner

Assessment of Learning

How do we judge successful teaching? Surely the obvious criterion is the degree of learning which has taken place. We looked in Chapter 3 at how learning could be brought about. Now we need to consider how we can measure the success of our strategies. The outcome of learning has been expressed in terms of a change in a student's behaviour which is relatively permanent and which can be ascertained from observation. *Assessment* is aimed at finding out what changes have occurred, and by this means enabling the teacher to see how much learning has taken place. By implication, it follows that assessment provides us with that measuring rod of our own success as teachers, at least with respect to our students' learning.

For these reasons, assessment should not be tagged on the end of our teaching, almost as an afterthought. Since our students' progress should be one of the main ways of judging our performance as teachers, assessment must be at the centre of our strategy. It's so easy to get bound up with what we, as the teachers, have to do, that we forget that it is what they, the students, can do after we have taught them, which really matters. To find out if we have been successful, we need reliable assessment methods.

Too often, students have only the haziest idea of their progress in a subject; the natural optimism of youth gives way to dissatisfaction at the 'poor teaching' when the student comes to grief in the 'terminal' examination. Of course the use of words such as 'terminal' or 'final' to describe examinations is educational nonsense and I'm glad that many courses now put far less emphasis on the 'judgement day' approach to assessing learning. Many courses now have an element of continuous assessment, which helps to underline the ongoing nature of learning; it has also eliminated some of the 'cramming' which made a mockery of some so-called courses of education. The administrative burden which continuous assessment places on teachers is worth bearing if it forces us to recognize the value of regular, formal assessment. Of course, the whole system can degenerate into meaningless paperwork, but it need not, given the enthusiastic and sensible cooperation of teachers.

Student Self-assessment and Spur-of-the-moment Exercises

Before dealing with formal assessment, let us consider the kind of assessment which teachers need to employ on a day-to-day basis in order to check understanding and progress. What I am suggesting here is something less formal and more integrated into the actual learning process. It involves the students' active participation in *self-assessment* which can motivate them to greater achievement.

When you are considering the next class's learning activities, try to choose activities which enable you to assess their learning, but more important, which enable the students to see for themselves what progress they have made and gain encouragement from it. At least once during every class (and it doesn't have to be at the end) you should set off some student activity which provides scope for assessment. In the old days we called these 'exercises', but the point of them was often lost on the students. Make the point of any exercise clear, if possible by showing how the required knowledge or skill is useful as life equipment, or if not, at least by demonstrating how it relates to the course programme. You won't always have time to prepare something in detail before the class, although as you gain experience you should be able to build up a repertoire of exercises. Careful preparation usually pays dividends, yet when you start teaching there are just too many classes to prepare for! Invest your time in providing a proper course programme and in keeping up with marking, but don't fret if you can't prepare for every class completely. Flexibility is important and this means the ability to react to the learning needs of the class and indeed to its mood.

Spur-of-the-moment exercises can be very beneficial. You have just explained a concept, skill or set of relationships. What do you do next? Dictate a note? Perhaps 20 per cent of the class will have fully mastered the explanation. Oh yes, if you ask them, 95 per cent will tell you they understand and if you say, 'Are there any questions?' (one of the most useless of all teaching techniques) 100 per cent silence will usually follow. No, you must get them to come to terms with the new knowledge or skill, to familiarize themselves with it. I hear the cry, 'There's no time!' – but what are you there for? – To teach your subject or to help your students learn it? Surely the latter is closer to the real purpose of your job. I'll return to the question of time, but your aim should be to see that time wastage is kept to the minimum; only rarely does the 'insufficient time' plea really stand up to close investigation.

So spend time *consolidating* students' learning by giving self-assessment exercises. It may be mental laziness on the teacher's part which causes the reluctance to indulge in such activities, but you must stir your imagination to come up with ideas. Teachers of skills will readily produce a multitude of different exercises to develop their students, but some knowledge-based teachers seem to lack imagination here. For instance, you have been explaining the two ways of classifying something. Instead of now giving a note summarizing what you have just said, which will probably only increase the confusion of at least half of those who didn't understand the first time, give your students a list of items and ask them to classify them in writing. Go round the room and quickly check every one, offering personal words of advice, encouragement and congratulation as appropriate. Personal contact in a large class must necessarily be brief, but it is vital for the communication of enthusiasm. You needn't check work in detail, but you must demonstrate that everyone is under your scrutiny. Don't embarrass students unduly if they have made a hash of things – ridicule and sarcasm should only be used very sparingly indeed, since they tend to rebound on their author. If one or two students have completely lost their way, it's better to give them a few minutes after the class ends, or arrange some suitable time outside class hours. If you try to explain again to them in front of the class, you not only make them feel inferior, but you also leave the rest of the students feeling bored. Above all, you are wasting teaching and learning time; better to be using your time to help the majority of your class, provided that you can give time to the minority before their next lesson.

Of course, if your feedback from the exercise is that the majority don't understand, you must go back. If you rush ahead ('I must cover the syllabus') you cannot claim to be a good teacher, any more than a bricklayer can claim professional competence if he doesn't bother to put right an uneven row of bricks before starting the next row. However, don't expect 100 per cent understanding and competence from your students; you may be surprised when you start teaching how little is grasped at the first encounter with a new topic. But if you think about it, this is common to everyday life; consider how often we need time, repetition and practice to familiarize ourselves with new things; for example, remember the confusion which resulted from the introduction of decimal currency in Britain.

Don't worry if a few students fall by the wayside during a lesson – you can do a first aid job on them later. It's up to your professional judgement to decide how far to pursue complete understanding; if it's a peripheral rather than a fundamental part of the subject, it may be acceptable that only a minority of the class grasp it. For a basic concept, your ideal should be 100 per cent, but in reality you must accept that you can only afford the time for possibly five minutes of extra help per student, and there may be one or two who do get left behind. Try to refer them to back-up material which may guide them through, such as a chapter of an easy-to-read textbook. If they have the motivation, they will persevere, but don't lose too much sleep over them. Resources are limited and if you have used those available to the best of your ability, you ought to accept the failures with equanimity, perhaps comforted by the thought that it is rare indeed for a student to have gained nothing from his or her course.

As enthusiastic teachers, we like to believe that we will be able to achieve the impossible where others have failed and obtain 100 per cent success. One of the hardest lessons the new teacher has to learn is that teaching is like other areas of life: it is not just black or white, and there are large grey areas of compromise. So we have to compromise over the degree of learning we can achieve in our students; we try to make their learning as effective as possible, but in the end we must appreciate that we are dealing with people – fallible, unpredictable people – and so we must be content with a satisfactory outcome to the learning process rather than a perfect one.

RECOGNIZE AND ACT ON LACK OF UNDERSTANDING

You may be able to recognize a lack of understanding even before exercises are done. With experience, you learn to pick up the tell-tale signs that you are not 'getting it across'. Students' expressions may change to frowns or puzzlement, but more often their eyes glaze over and somehow you know it's going over their heads. If they can no longer follow the argument, their attention will wander, so that even those students who usually follow you by maintaining eye contact start looking around, doodling or fidgeting in some other way. If this becomes general, you must do something about it: halt your explanation at a convenient point that doesn't look too obvious and then change the activity for a short time. It may be sufficient if you call for two minutes' break, so students can stretch themselves and relax. You can then go back over the material which was giving difficulty, preferably trying to explain it in a simpler way. A better method is to try to get students to grasp what you are explaining by means of a simple off-the-cuff exercise. The very act of having to find a piece of scrap paper and copy something off the board, say, is in itself a change of activity and to that extent a break. (Incidentally, students should be encouraged to keep a notebook for 'rough work'. Too many have what I call the 'tablets of stone' mentality: they only want to put the final 'authorized version' in their notes and are therefore inhibited from experimenting and trying things out for themselves.)

CHALLENGING EXERCISES

You must be ready to dream up something for your students to do at any point in the lesson, just to stir their concentration and try to get your point across. Most students like a challenge, so use your ingenuity; what about getting students to work in pairs on a problem involving a simple scenario described verbally by you? Or set an individual challenge by putting a short exercise on the board which gives practice in what has just been learnt and preferably pushes out the frontiers of knowledge and competence just that little bit further. The questions raised by the exercise can then act as the springboard for the next portion of the lesson. Exercises can involve a brief piece of practical work using apparatus, or oral contributions to a discussion; try to vary the activities to keep your students on their toes – try to create an atmosphere of anticipation in your classes (but don't overdo things, or you will bring about apprehension instead).

EXPLAIN PROBLEM AREAS AGAIN

These activities should give you feedback on any stumbling blocks to learning. Once you are aware of the problem, go back and deal with it. But be careful not to repeat word-for-word your previous explanation; try to approach from a slightly different angle. If you can't do this, the chances are that you have not fully mastered your subject – you are limited to the approach adopted by the textbook you read last night! Only if you have an all-round knowledge of your subject will you be able to teach it from different angles. Good teaching technique is no substitute for properly knowing your subject. True, if I had to choose between good subject mastery and good teaching technique, I would not hesitate to plump for the latter, but of course the best teachers have both!

BENEFITS OF INFORMAL ASSESSMENT

The benefits of exercises, whether planned or unplanned, are many. They break up a lesson, introducing a different form of learning activity. They give an opportunity for more two-way communication, either as you discuss the exercise with individual students, or as you invite students to tell the rest of the class how they have completed the exercise. What is more, informal assessment of this type does not have to involve giving marks or grades; a piano teacher listens to a student playing a piece and then assesses the performance informally: that part was a little too loud, put more expression into these phrases, and so on. The word 'assessment' comes from the Latin, meaning 'to sit beside', and there could be no better description of our purpose in using assessment to benefit our students' learning. Above all, informal assessment encourages *student involvement*; too much of our teaching washes over the heads of students day after day. It's worrying to think of the waste of resources involved, yet we as teachers (and I count myself guilty of this on many occasions) do not always take the trouble to see that our efforts – or more precisely those of our students – are channelled into the most effective learning activities.

Formal Assessment

Your approach to formal assessment should be on a more long-term basis which covers the whole course. This may already be available in a laid-down programme of in-course assignment work, continuously assessed, or it may be determined by the needs of a traditional final examination. The GCSE has brought a breath of fresh air to our classrooms, yet it has laid a heavy burden of coursework assessment on teachers. More than ever, we are being obliged to give this aspect of our teaching the time and effort it deserves. Even if there is no predetermined assessment structure for a course, you are hardly doing a complete teaching job if you don't arrange for regular, recorded assessment of students' performance.

The main objects of this approach are to *monitor* and *validate* students' progress. In practical terms, this implies that you should regard formal assessment as a means of motivating your students throughout the course by providing them with a series of goals to aim for, and as a means of giving them regular practice in carrying out tasks similar to those they will have to perform by the end of the course to demonstrate their competence.

MOTIVATION

Let us consider the motivation aspect first. Now provided that a majority of the students are well motivated, it may be that the remainder will be persuaded to try harder by the desire to conform; they don't want to be seen to be lower achievers than their fellow students. Natural competitive desires may also play a part in this process of motivation. However, like many teaching techniques, this one has drawbacks. If nearly all the students lack motivation, there is pressure to conform to the uncooperative stance of the majority, so your ploy is likely to fail. Competition in education is a controversial subject; it can be argued that individualism should not be taken to the point where it makes students ruthless and selfish. I certainly do not go in for placings of students – their order in the class – following an assessment. We would however be naive to believe that our students do not compare their relative performances, and I would suggest that this desire to 'keep up with the Joneses' in an educational sense, whether it is a good thing in itself or not, should be harnessed in the interests of learning.

Incidentally, you should be aware that there is often a 'U-shape effect' with students' motivation: they start off keenly, then gradually lose interest until the exams approach, when they suddenly decide to do some work. Unfortunately, this is often too late; exam success would be more easily and reliably achieved if there had been a sustained effort. There is no easy answer to this mid-year sag – you can try to design your course programme to avoid having the more tedious parts of the syllabus at this time, but they've got to go in some time – not at the end, and not at the beginning, so that only leaves the middle! Some sort of mid-session test or exam may serve to gee things up, although poor results may have the effect of further depressing and demotivating your students. So try to produce tests which give them some sense of achievement, while reminding them of the work they still have to do to reach their ultimate goal. This is easier said than done, but if you can maintain your own enthusiasm and momentum, this will help drag your students through their Slough of Despond, and enable you to give them worthwhile assessments. It may seem like sheer slog, both for you and them, but it's part of your job to acquaint students with the fact that quite a lot of life does fall into this category; the ability to literally 'stay the course' is a valuable one.

The key to making the most of formal assessment is to give it some *status* in the students' eyes; if they think it matters, they will stir themselves to achieve better results. Assessment should therefore be part of the regular learning pattern, not something haphazard; it should appear to be carefully planned in advance. (Notice that this does not prevent your spur-of-the-moment exercises playing their full part in your teaching strategies.) A series of tests enables you to gauge students' progress, especially if the tests are of comparable difficulty or are graded in some way.

Students like a regular routine, so having a weekly slot for a test is one way to help them into their own learning routine. Try to make a good job of producing any tests on paper; the more official they look, the more seriously they will be taken by students. Indicate clearly how marks are allocated and what the students are expected to do to earn them. It is a good idea to consider carefully your assessment criteria and set these out on the test paper; the same procedure can be used in assignments for continuous assessment purposes. If your students know the criteria on which you are judging their work, and the standards of achievement required to reach certain grades, they may be spurred on to better performance; they will at least be in a better position to understand and accept the marks or grades they receive. For formal assessment, it is only fair to give reasonable notice so that students can prepare properly; after all, one of the main reasons for the exercise is to encourage students to do some work on their own. By the same token, you should not be persuaded to postpone a test by a few lazy students who haven't done their homework. Obviously, if a majority of the students are absent at the appointed time, you may have postponement forced on you, but this should be exceptional. You want your students to believe that if you say there will be a test next Friday, you mean it.

Record Assessments to Monitor Performance

Once you have recorded a series of marks or grades over a time period, you will be able to monitor performance and progress in a more precise and objective manner. Teachers' impressions of their students' progress are not always reliable, especially when dealing with a large class where there is little time for individual attention. Proper recorded assessments help you to build up a profile of each student's progress, and pin-point those students whose performance gives cause for concern. Experience shows that some students drift through courses without ever being brought up short and confronted with their poor performance; inevitably, they either fail to reach the required standard at the end of the course, or at the very least do not take full advantage of what the course had to offer.

Act Quickly on Assessment Results

To make the most out of formal assessment, you must therefore ensure that tests are marked, returned and followed up *quickly*. In this way your students gain the maximum benefit from them.

General points can be explained to the whole class, but individual problems must be tackled separately, probably by personal tuition at the end of the lesson or at some other mutually convenient time. The whole idea is to prevent students 'freewheeling', marking time on a course rather than contributing and learning. You will be very lucky indeed to have a class absolutely full of self-motivated students; sociologists can argue over why this is such a rare event, but as teachers we have to face reality, day after day. So do try to use assessment constructively to encourage your students to participate in their progress.

ASSESSMENT TO PREPARE FOR FINAL EXAMINATIONS

The second aspect of formal assessment is as a means of *practice* and *preparation* for any final examination or other test of competence to which the course is leading. 'Practice, practice, practice!' used to be the cry, but now that rote learning has gone out of fashion, somehow it has also become not quite the done thing to get students to do lots of repetitive exercises. This is unfortunate, because active learning is nearly always better than the passive type. If you are charged with the job of preparing your students for some final examination or test, you should do this properly, and there is no better way than making them carry out similar tasks under similar conditions. For instance, many students are still faced with the traditional essay question in examinations, yet many will not do justice to themselves because they have not had sufficient practice in this method of communication. Essays written as homework, with no constraints on time or access to information, do not give the right kind of practice. I prefer to ask students to use their homework time to prepare a topic, and then check that they have done the work by giving them an essay question to answer under exam conditions in class. In this way, they can learn by their mistakes – one of the oldest and most effective of all methods – but they will be making the mistakes now rather than in the examination. I will return to this in the next section.

Objective tests and multiple choice come into many assessments these days. They are popular with most students, who can appreciate the element of challenge which is more obvious than with an essay question. Also, a wider area of the syllabus can be assessed, and they can usually be marked more quickly than essays. However, they do take time to devise and produce, so if you can find a book with suitable questions, an investment in a class set is worthwhile. If the examination includes questions in this form, it is vital that you prepare your students adequately. As with essay writing, there is a certain amount of technique which can be picked up with practice and familiarity, so make sure that your students are fully conversant with every type of problem that the examiners can throw at them.

ASSESSMENT TO GIVE A COURSE VALIDITY

What about courses where there are no laid-down aims in terms of final examinations and/or continuous assessment to be met? Formal assessment gives some validity to the course in students' eyes; there is no doubt that the absence of any recognized goals does have an effect on students' perception of the course; they may regard the class as a 'fill-in', with little relevance to their mainstream work. This is no problem if you are teaching mature people who appreciate the value of learning for its own sake, but some younger students are impatient with any lessons which do not seem relevant to their immediate aims in life. The more tangible and obvious you can make the advantages of the course, the better. In these circumstances, you will need to substitute your own goals for outside ones; it's often difficult to get homework out of these students, so use your lesson time to get them involved in a variety of projects which you assess and they keep as evidence of their endeavours. If they see that you carefully assess and record the work done, they will at least feel that there is some meaning to the whole affair, and you can always say that you will be submitting a report to their course tutor based on the results they achieve.

Homework

I have mentioned homework a number of times, so perhaps it is appropriate to be more prescriptive about this contentious subject. The best approach to homework I have found is to ask oneself, 'How does it contribute to my students' learning, and to my assessment of that learning?' There are two points here. First, there are many circumstances where homework can contribute to students' learning: looking up reference books, working on a project, carrying out a survey, reworking notes taken in class, and many more. I don't like to see homework being given where there should have been adequate class time for all the necessary learning activities. If that time has been frittered away by inefficient teaching, it is unfair to expect students to make it up in their own time. It is even worse if homework is set simply because the school or college authorities say it must be. Surely coursework done outside timetabled hours should be allotted according to the learning requirements of the course, rather than because of some administrative decree? Nevertheless, teachers are sometimes faced with these realities, and, as always, have to make the best of them.

HOMEWORK AS A PREPARATION FOR CLASSWORK

If you are faced with a requirement to set a certain number of homeworks, treat it as an opportunity to widen the scope of your students' learning. I have already referred to setting preparation work to be followed up by a class activity – after all, homework is still called 'prep' in many schools. The activity to follow the homework can be some sort of test for assessment purposes, but equally it could be group work. The latter can help to make homework seem more relevant to the student; he or she is made responsible for preparing one portion of an activity to be pursued on a group basis in class. If a student fails to do his or her prep, the censure of the group will be far more effective than any sanctions you can threaten. Homework then becomes a vehicle for widening your students' horizons rather than mere drudgery; since it becomes a preparation for actual work done in class, help from parents is transformed from being cheating to a valuable form of assistance.

HOMEWORK FOR ASSESSMENT PURPOSES

The second point arising from our original question concerns the value of homework for assessment purposes. This revolves around the validity we can attach to assessment of work which is done under such a variety of conditions. Ignoring the help students may receive from their parents, how can we compare work done by a student under difficult conditions, sharing the living room with a noisy family, with work done by a student in his or her own room under ideal conditions? Surely the only fair approach is to carry out most assessment under conditions of equality in the classroom. Of course, you cannot ensure that the prep is done under the same conditions, but at least you are going some way towards compensating for different home environments. You can assess either group or individual work on a much fairer basis if it is undertaken in class, and there is the added advantage that you have all the work available for marking at the same time. You will be spared the aggravation of having to put up with some students handing it in late, accompanied by a kaleidoscopic variety of more or less plausible excuses; this will save you all the time, hassle and paper shuffling which arise from having to chase up outstanding work and mark it separately.

PRACTICAL POINTS FOR SETTING HOMEWORK

There is a very useful free book about homework – including a survey – published by Her Majesty's Inspectors in the 'Education Observed' series, which is worth consulting. A few practical points of my own follow now. Don't set homework right at the end of the lesson when students are rushing to leave the class; a lot of bad homework happens because students fail to understand what is required of them. This presupposes of course that you have planned the homework in advance; it looks very bad if you have to scratch around for something in front of the class. Give clear instructions, and preferably write them on the board. State the date by which the work must be handed in, or if it involves prep for classwork, fix a date there and then for the follow-up activity, and write it in your teaching file so that there can be no argument later. If you are planning some sort of test or exercise which will need marking, try to arrange the date so that you will have sufficient time to complete the marking before the following lesson. This isn't always possible if a strict homework timetable is in force, but if you can arrange for heavy marking loads to be gathered in just before you have some free marking time, this will help to get the marked work returned at the earliest opportunity, with a consequent improvement in feedback effectiveness. In practice, this may mean that you take home a lot of weekend marking; I only know of one profession which carries home larger briefcases than teachers, and that is the turf accountants – their rewards are certainly more tangible than teachers', but perhaps not so satisfying!

Marking

While trying to see that our students are usefully occupied, we must equally make sure that our own time and effort is used effectively. This is where some teachers fall down. In the classroom they may be 'naturals'. Outside it, having to deal with avalanches of paperwork, they are sunk. Teachers who have had previous office experience are at a distinct advantage here, and paper-shifting techniques, originally devised for the office, can easily be adapted to educational establishments.

VALUE AND IMPORTANCE OF MARKING

The more that your subject is concerned with written knowledge rather than physical skills (typewriting is an exception here), the more paper you will have for marking. Now let's be clear straight away about the value and importance of marking; its object is to assess students' work to see if learning is taking place, and to show students how to improve their work by example and encouragement. So you must give marking a high priority (yes, I know, along with all those other things that had to be done yesterday!). But realistically, you should rank preparation and assessment (marking) as of equal importance if you are going to produce a balanced teaching performance. Students may find it difficult to judge your quality as a class teacher, but they will easily compare your marking efficiency with that of other teachers. Educationally, the sooner a student has a response to his or her work, the more useful it is; work returned weeks after it has been handed in loses all impact, and going through it is like trying to breathe life into a corpse. If students see you taking ages to return work, they will grant themselves extra time to do it, and as with punctuality, no amount of threats can compensate for a poor example on your part. Also, you will find it hard to keep tabs on laggards who really are falling into arrears with handing in work; if you don't get round to some marking for weeks, what hope have you of sorting out those falling behind, when so much time has already passed? They will get further and further behind, either becoming disheartened or giving up altogether. Your job is to nip this problem in the bud, counselling students as required. Some may have genuine difficulties, often a family problem, which demands your sympathetic help by way of extending deadlines so that a breathing space is provided. Many students simply do not appreciate the importance of getting something done on time, yet this is often vital for holding down a job in the outside world. To the vague excuse, 'I didn't have enough time', I reply that we all have the same amount of time, 24 hours in each day, but we must give priority to those tasks which must be completed by a certain date. You must be flexible and understanding in dealing with less mature students, but don't let them think they can get away with handing in work late without a satisfactory explanation, otherwise you will be making a rod for your own back, just as with lateness. In practice, it's difficult to avoid a small proportion of late work, but it means extra bother for you in having to handle the paperwork separately and having to cast your mind back to remember what the exercise was all about. You will also have the problem of trying to achieve parity of marking level without the other papers being to hand, so there's the risk of under- or over-marking. Incidentally, quite a good deterrent to late handing in of work is to have a scale of downgrading for late submission, although this can be self-defeating for persistent offenders. In my records, I always underline marks which are the result of a late submission. This is a useful means of checking on students falling behind, and provides valuable data for the compiling of reports on the students concerned.

STUDENTS WHO FALL BEHIND WITH COURSEWORK

What if a student starts to fall behind with coursework, and you cannot get any satisfaction after repeated private words? Check with other teachers and the course tutor; if the problem is a general one it should be the responsibility of the tutor or other senior member of staff to try to help the student sort him or herself out. Don't let such matters slide; it's easy when there's so much to do to put off coming to grips with 'difficult' cases, but you are storing up trouble for yourself if you let the matter of a problem student drag on. Often, the student is his or her own worse enemy, adopting an uncooperative and apathetic attitude which does not encourage members of staff to be helpful. If you have personal responsibility as a course tutor for a student's progress, you must make every effort within reason to achieve a positive outcome, perhaps by arranging a special meeting with parents if appropriate, or by referral to a more skilled counsellor than yourself. If your responsibility does not extend beyond your subject, try to see that whoever *is* responsible is galvanized into action. In education, quite a lot of nagging is needed to get things done, so don't be afraid to make a nuisance of yourself if you believe in your cause. If you do find yourself banging your head against a brick wall, it's wise to cover yourself by putting your misgivings in writing, sending a dated note to the responsible teacher and keeping a copy. Sometimes, problem students can cause quite nasty ructions later on if they turn on their teachers and blame them for their failure; you need to show that you did everything within your power to try to help. Even if you are the responsible teacher, there are limits to the time you can spend on such students; don't let them monopolize your time – keep the matter in perspective. This is why it's vital to bring the problem out into the open and settle it quickly, rather than letting it run on for months on end, distracting you from performing effectively, to the detriment of the great majority of your students. So try to get the senior staff on your side in making positive decisions about a student's future; if he or she is put 'on probation', insist that subsequent progress is carefully monitored, and if not of an acceptable standard, decisions are made rapidly. We can't be too sentimental when we are dealing with hundreds of students: we try to be sympathetic, we do all that our time and energy will allow; ultimately, however, we must try to achieve the greatest good for the greatest number of our students. On many occasions, if we are on the ball and deal swiftly with a problem before it gets out of hand, these considerations will not apply, but now and again we must deal justly but ruthlessly with students, who, for whatever reason, cannot or will not do the course work.

MARKING SYSTEMS

Teachers have their own pet marking systems, but you should choose one which is:

(a) simple to understand by students;
(b) can be aggregated, averaged or whatever for the purpose of reports, etc;
(c) bears some relationship to the way the course is officially assessed – eg if you are preparing for examinations where each question is marked out of 20, it makes sense to use that as a reference mark, but where grades are required for in-course assessment, it's best to use A, B, C etc throughout.

You would be wise to consult your colleagues on suitable marking practice; there may already be one laid down by your institution, or prescribed by an examination board or other external body.

Always try to remember that marks are supposed to record progress, and that marking gives you the opportunity both to encourage and to warn. You must be awfully careful to be fair; there is the well-documented 'halo effect', which makes teachers give higher marks to students perceived by them as being 'good'. Likewise, 'bad' students may be damned in the teacher's mind before marking begins. You cannot avoid these effects, but you can be aware of them and ensure that you are scrupulous in being fair; however, don't go over the top and over-compensate. Try to mark a set of work at one sitting in order to achieve consistency; this is why you need to have all work in together. I have the impression that if I only look at one or two pieces at a time spread over several days, I end up with very uneven marking. It's not always possible to mark in one sitting, of course, and it's more important to return the stuff quickly, so if you can't mark all in one go, have a quick review when you do finish to check that there are no glaring inconsistencies. I pencil in my mark to begin with, then when I have read all the scripts and am satisfied over the consistency of my marking, I ink in the marks and at the same time note them in my records. If a student does discover a marking mistake or any other inconsistency, don't be rushed into changing marks there and then unless you are convinced of the correctness of the claim; promise to take the paper away for quiet reflection, so that any further errors can be avoided, and an equitable settlement arrived at.

If you review work submitted, you have a better chance of discovering the lazy students who copy off others. This generally happens more with work submitted late, so be on your guard; crafty students may delay the submission of homework in order to copy off marked and returned work. As with crime, the threat of detection is probably more of a deterrent than any punishment meted out afterwards, so make your students aware that you know when it goes on. It's not always easy to know who is copying off whom, so I sometimes halve the marks between the two students. If one confesses, you can try to get him or her to do another separate piece of work, but this is not always realistic. Usually, if you make it clear that you strongly disapprove of copying, and explain the poor educational rewards of the practice, you will obtain the reluctant cooperation of most students.

You will probably have learnt that impression marking generally gives results quite close to those of more precise methods, and with practice you will find it a useful way of ploughing through all the work handed in, provided your subject is amenable to the method. If you maintain the habit of reviewing your marking as you go along for the sake of consistency, you won't go far wrong. Another way is to mark just a random sample of papers submitted. Go through these carefully to see if satisfactory learning is taking place, and if there are any common difficulties. The remaining papers can simply be checked to see that the work has been done. Now obviously you need to assemble a comprehensive set of marks to assess the progress of every student; there are however occasions when you simply want to check that students do the work that you have set. If you tried to mark in detail all the work set you would never have time to do anything else; it is important to apportion your time sensibly between marking and preparation. If you find that all your free time is taken up with marking, not only will your lessons suffer, but you will become increasingly frustrated by the never-ending treadmill of it all. So use impression marking and random samples now and again to help you cope with the marking load; you can use them when you receive the answers to the holiday background reading questions you set, as suggested in the previous chapter.

For ordinary homework and other exercises, I usually pick out what I expect to be the best papers, and mark them first. Cynics would say that this is to provide me with the correct answers, so that I can mark the rest, but if you can see what standard has been reached by your best students, you can grade the less gifted more easily. If even your best students have not done well, you need to review your teaching methods and the nature of the work set. For the marking of serious examinations (are there any other sort?), I put the papers into alphabetical name order and mark one question at a time to try to obtain consistency for each question. Any queries about an overall result can then be dealt with by rereading the whole paper through and marking impressionistically, although it's probably better to erase your marks and pass the paper to a colleague for an independent assessment.

I usually mark in green ink, because green is a psychologically positive colour in contrast to red. The whole thrust of educational development these days is to encourage the student in what he or she can *achieve*, and to provide profiles, certificates and diplomas on that basis. So in our marking we should be reinforcing by encouragement the good things in students' work, rather than just penalizing the bad. When marking, teachers tend to pick out the obvious mistakes – especially spelling – because they feel constrained to make some marks on the paper. It's often more difficult and time-consuming to write a concise criticism of the actual text – why you only gave it C+ – but this will be more helpful than a paper covered with red marks and having the cryptic comment, 'Fair' scribbled at the bottom. By all means draw a student's attention to poor spelling if it's really spoiling his or her work, but a more useful ploy is to let students know that you will focus on different aspects of their work at different times: one week you might concentrate on presentation, another on analytical skills. Eschew the nit-picking attitude of some teachers, who give little positive encouragement to their students. Any word of encouragement, however small, can help a student, but don't emulate one of my teachers, who had written on the first piece of work submitted by a new student he had never taught before, 'A great improvement'! As you mark, keep a note on a separate sheet of the main points to which you wish to draw your students' attention. If you can then go through these matters in class when you hand the work back, it will save you duplicating a detailed explanation on each individual paper.

RETURNING WORK TO STUDENTS

Try to return all work personally, making appropriate comments, but not holding the student up to public ridicule. I like to regard returning work as a personal one-to-one affair, so I do it privately, so far as this is possible in the classroom situation. This personal contact is important – someone is taking a personal interest in the student's progress, or lack of it. Most students respond to personal interest; if you need to make more than a few spoken words of comment, have a word afterwards. You can return marked work at the beginning of the lesson, to get it out of the way, or leave it to halfway through, so that there is a small change of activity and a natural break. Always try to explain what you expected for a good piece of work – indeed you should have indicated this properly when you set it. Draw the class's attention to any widespread problems which arose, and try to make sure that your students learn from their mistakes. Any humorous mistakes in work being handed back can be shared with the class, provided that the writer's anonymity is respected and you know that he or she can join in the fun with the rest of the class. There are some students who really feel that everything they submit must be absolutely perfect, so in their striving for perfection they often fall behind in their work. Mistakes are actually good if they help students to learn, so get your students into a positive frame of mind so that they are willing to risk mistakes in order to learn. Remind them of the old saying, 'The person who has never made a mistake has never made anything.'

Reports, References and Profiles

REPORTS

Reports are another paperwork nightmare for some teachers. The secret here is to have adequate records of results and marks so that you can refer to them to help you make reasonably objective comments about a student. Again, education is changing, so that the old, bland clichés such as 'could do better' are now frowned upon. Yet if we did not believe that most students could do better, could make progress, could achieve more, we would hardly be in the teaching profession. So, much of what we say in reports must come down to stating progress so far – either good or bad – and then exhorting greater effort in the future. Even if it is a 'final' report, there should be no finality in education; we must always be looking ahead, encouraging every student to go forward from where they are now. For these reasons, it is worth investing time in report writing; if the words simply won't come, try starting with a word such as 'Although . . . ' or 'Despite . . . '. This frequently seems to trigger off a response in one's mind and helps provide a balanced comment: 'Although John has been conscientious this year and has shown interest in the course, he will find the second year much more taxing academically, so should be prepared for extra effort in order to achieve the success he deserves.' We are encouraging John by praising him for his hard work and saying that he deserves to succeed, but at the same time helping him to recognize the truth that his gifts are limited, and so urging him to put even more effort into his second year. Another way to jog your memory is to keep a list of 'buzz words': words which you use repeatedly in report writing, and which may set off a fruitful train of thought when you sit facing a blank report form. Occasionally, you need to be brutally frank in reports, but try to make even these constructive rather than destructive: 'It's a pity that Fiona has been so lazy and uninterested in this subject, because she could make a valuable contribution to the class if she felt more willing to be involved.' Here, we are stating the unpalatable facts, but are still trying to bring the lost sheep back to the fold.

REFERENCES
It should be rare indeed that we have to wash our hands completely of a student, and even then we may expect that time will help in the process of maturing and mellowing, if not reform. On one occasion I had to write a reference for a student who had been asked to leave because she refused to cooperate and carry out the work that the course entailed. I could only state the truth in her reference, because it would undermine the value of references if I

did not. You have a responsibility to your educational institution and indeed to society as a whole, as well as to your students, so it's no good inflicting a totally unsuitable person on another organization. Ultimately, you are acting in your student's best interests, because a worthwhile career cannot be built upon lies. It's well known that references are read more for what they don't say than for what they include, but try to be as objective and realistic as you can when writing them. By all means emphasize the good points and play down the weaknesses, but don't be afraid to speak your mind – this gives a ring of authenticity to the reference. Taken with a good interview, it can persuade an employer that the candidate is 'worth a chance'. I once gave a reference to a bank in which I said that the student, while having many good qualities, did lack maturity. Perhaps this stood out among all the other cautious, non-committal references for other candidates, because, after the expected good interview, my student got the job.

INFORMATION RECORDS
I have said that it helps if you keep records of your students' performance accessible. These, and registers of class attendance, are the basic records you will use (with your mental perception of the student) to produce reports and references. The more objective information you have to hand, the easier it should be to comment accurately and constructively on a particular student. So try to record all the assessment data you can – any test or exercise marks which give a useful indication of progress and achievement. Taken in isolation, they may not mean much, but collected over a term or a year, they provide a pattern which could lead to further enquiry and sorting out of some impediment to progress.

PROFILES
Profiles are being used increasingly to record students' progress. Their object is to describe exactly what a student has done during a course, and can do at the end of it. They are thus records of achievement, and may be regarded as valuable documents for the students concerned. Their compilation requires the keeping of detailed records, so you see that it is more necessary than ever to take record keeping seriously. I don't think that profiles will ever replace references – indeed, profiles are usually accompanied by some sort of testimonial – but they are a step in the right direction to the extent that they acknowledge that we are in the business of *achievement* by our students, and that this should be recognized

formally. It is also good that the students themselves can make contributions to their own profiles, giving their reactions to their school or college and commenting on what they have learnt. Having expressed these sentiments, I should point out the disadvantage of profiles. It's easy to get diverted from our primary responsibility of facilitating learning into a morass of bureaucracy; don't let the extra paperwork involved ruin your teaching. Pieces of paper are only as good as the students who hold them, so concentrate on the students' achievement through learning, and let the profiles accurately reflect this rather than be an end in themselves.

Records of Attendance and Work

ATTENDANCE REGISTERS

Attendance registers can help to indicate trends of motivation. It's surprising how often your impressions of a student's attendance turn out to be quite misleading – you may not notice really quite substantial absence, or you could erroneously believe that a student has had many more absences than is in fact the case. The register will reveal any pattern of absence which may help you diagnose the problem; this will show up in a way that is not possible from casual mental notes of absences. The obvious minimum requirement from one of your students is that he or she at least turns up regularly for your lessons. A detailed attendance record, showing substantial absence, or even just the missing of some of the more vital lessons, is valuable evidence when you are called upon to explain a student's poor performance. Of course, you have only covered yourself if you took what steps you could to draw these matters to the attention of the appropriate authorities – course tutor, form teacher, head of year, etc, although you will usually start by personally tackling the student (when he or she turns up!). It's so easy to let such matters slide, but time is the enemy here; the weeks slip by, and before you know where you are, a crisis has blown up, perhaps with the student panicking at the rapid approach of exams, and pleading for extra tuition. As with other breaches of discipline, skipping classes should be dealt with as soon after the event as possible. Make the effort to catch up with students and tackle them about absences. Don't however go in for an undignified chase around school or college – this will only encourage them to play games of hide-and-seek. If you can't sort the student out satisfactorily, make sure you notify the authorities in writing – and keep a copy!

RECORDS OF WORK

Your own personal record of work is an indispensable part of the educational paperwork. The object is to keep a permanent record of what you did – and, more important, of what the students did – in every class. Consider the benefits of this: you can refer back to see what teaching and learning strategies you employed last year, and take account of any comments you recorded on their effectiveness. As well as this, you can see how long it took to cover a particular part of the syllabus, and take this into account when producing your course programme. The records can also be consulted when some query arises over whether some skill or item of knowledge has already been dealt with; if you have several similar classes, it's very easy to get them mixed up, and you can't always rely on the students to set you right.

I run off a standard record-of-work sheet, and keep a separate copy in my loose-leaf teaching file for each class I teach. I have gradually refined the design over the years to suit my requirements, and the example given opposite is my latest effort.

The total number in the group is useful not only for the head count at the start of lessons, but also for reminding you how many copies of a handout to produce. I like to put down the week number, to tie in with my programme of work (more on this shortly). The space for lesson notes is not regularly filled in with the sort of plans we prepared at training college – there wouldn't be room anyway! – but is mainly used to put in notes and reminders about what should be done during the lesson: to see a certain student about absence, to remind the class about exam entries, and so on. However, there are occasions when I need to plan the structure of my lessons more carefully; then I use the space to sketch a simple lesson plan which acts as an *aide-mémoire* during the lesson itself. You can keep a note of when you set homework, what it was and when it is due in, thus preventing those regular disputes with students who insist that, 'You said you didn't want it in until next week!' Finally, you summarize on the sheet what has happened during that particular lesson: knowledge or skills dealt with, exercises done, and any special points worth noting for future reference, such as whether a particular learning strategy was successful. This needn't be more than two or three lines at the most, and you should fill it in immediately the lesson is over,

Course Code:			Course Tutor:		No. in class:		
Date of lesson D | M		Notes for class	Week No.	Record of work	Homework/ assignment set	Date due in D | M	

before you get up from your desk and leave the classroom. Very often, time is short, and you must be up and away to another room; you may also wish to see one or two students at the end of the lesson, and others may want to speak to you. It's always best to deal with these matters on the spot if you can, but unless you have free time ahead, it's usually wise first of all to take a minute to complete your record of work before the next lesson makes you forget what you did. Besides, you have your file open at the right place and probably some headings written on the board, so take advantage of the circumstances to keep your records up to date. Frequently, there will be students pressing to enter the room for the next lesson. Unless I am remaining in the room for that lesson, I insist that all my students (including any I speak to after the lesson) have left the room before I permit the next lot in. If their teacher is with them, you must of course cooperate courteously, but often groups of younger students think they can barge their way into classrooms without any regard for common courtesy, so don't be intimidated – stand your ground; ask them firmly to please remain outside, and then finish dealing with your students and completing your record of work.

Use a Teaching File

I put my record of work sheets on the right hand side of my teaching file, and then on the opposite side I place copies of my programme of work. So when I go into a class, I can open my teaching file and see at a glance what the programme has planned for that particular week and also what we did last lesson, with any notes on plans for this lesson, students to be seen, homework to be set or collected, and so on. By having all this information available instantly as you enter a classroom, you are given extra confidence, and don't have to waste time fumbling around and asking limply 'Where did we get up to?' You will find that reference is made easier if you fix finger tabs to each section of your file dealing with a different class – colours are easier to recognize than a letter code, especially if you get used to the colours by using the same ones each year. I attach the coloured tab to the programme of work page, so that I can open my file to reveal that programme on the left and the current record of work sheet on the right; as I fill in these sheets they are placed below the current one in the file. Other documents relating to the class – class lists, exam entry form copies, documents concerning particular students – can be kept in the same section of your file below the records of work. You end up with a file divided into sections for each class. By the end of the year it will be almost full, and then you can transfer all the papers to a more permanent file. I often have need to refer back one or two years to see what exercises I set, or to dig out an old course programme which now needs revamping. Kept in order of year by your desk, these files provide invaluable records of the good (and the bad) features of your teaching. Take my tip that good record keeping is a worthwhile investment of your time and effort, giving you that more professional touch.

Timetables and Time Management

TIMETABLES
Timetables are part of our paperwork; we are ruled by them, having to appear in various places at various times of the week. Until you have learnt your timetable off by heart, you need to have it in an easily readable and accessible form. I copy mine onto a piece of card about five-and-a-half inches long by three-and-a-half inches wide, using a small self-adhesive label for each lesson slot, with the same colour code as on my teaching file tabs. I can then extract the card from my pocket with one hand while walking along the corridor carrying some files in my other hand. If you have your timetable sheet in the front of your teaching file, you will have to put everything down to open your file; if it is folded up in a pocket or handbag, you waste time unfolding it each time, and you will need to do this a good many times until you have learnt it. When planning my day, I sit at my desk, prop my timetable card up in front of me and try to work out how everything I want to do can be fitted in!

SCHOOL CALENDARS
It is also a good idea to have full details of your school or college calendar noted in your diary. Despite the well-known fact that long holidays are provided for teachers so that they can enjoy their nervous breakdowns in private, you will need to refer to a calendar for planning both before and during your courses. Initial planning of the course programme will have been based on the calendar, but as you go through the year, you will have to refer regularly to the programme to see if you are ahead of or behind time, and to anticipate half-terms, public holidays, and other annoying distractions (or welcome reliefs!). This is where giving each week

113

of your programme of work an actual date will help you, because you then avoid having to make endless calculations to see what number week you are supposed to be at. Your students also appreciate being able to pin their programme down to actual dates. So superimpose your school or college calendar on the one in your diary, and also write in the week numbers. You will then be able to compare course programme and diary when setting dates for the handing in of homework, assignments and projects.

TIME MANAGEMENT

All this emphasis on timetables and calendars may appear super-fluous, but you must appreciate how vital time management is for the teacher. I hope you won't turn into one of those teachers who waste time every day moaning to their colleagues about all the things they have to do, instead of getting on with them. Some teachers never provide themselves with an adequate framework of realistic course planning, so they are forever 'at sea' with their teaching, complaining of having to carry out a sort of permanent holding operation, and often struggling to catch up as exams approach. Many quite experienced teachers consider that detailed time-planning of courses is impracticable, but with more and more courses taking on an integrated nature, and with more team teaching, teachers increasingly need to keep in step with each other. I believe that in most subjects a competent teacher can keep fairly accurately to a course programme, barring unpredictable events such as the cancellation of a series of lessons; public holidays are predictable! Not only will good time management give you more confidence, but also it will impress your students, who like to feel that they are, to coin a phrase, 'on course'.

YOUR TIME OUTSIDE THE CLASSROOM

What of the management of your time outside the classroom? If you're not careful, those precious free periods or 'non-contact times' get frittered away. Those complaints from staff about insufficient time lead me to make three comments. First, teaching is an open-ended commitment, so we are never going to reach the stage where we can sit back and say we have done everything we can for our students; we have to do the best we can, given the available time, energy and resources; this must be recognized and accepted by every new, idealistic young teacher. Second, we ought to regard the hours for which we are paid but do not have to appear in front of students, as hours to be used effectively to further our teaching effort. We can compare these hours to the resources the army uses for its back-up effort: supplies, catering, medical, signals and engineers – these all follow behind the 'sharp end' of the fighting men, yet without them the soldiers' effectiveness would rapidly vanish. So look upon these 'spare' hours as the 'back-up' resource for your actual teaching efforts, and extract the most out of them. In your first few years of teaching, you're bound to have to sacrifice quite a lot of your personal time in lesson preparation and marking, simply because you're new to the game, but remember that the more effectively you use your paid hours, the less of your personal time you need to forego.

DEALING WITH PAPERWORK

My third comment is on the need for some teachers to learn how to deal effectively with paperwork. Even some of those who used to earn a living in offices seem to have no idea how to run an efficient desk. Go into staff-rooms, and what do you see? – piles of papers, folders and books, all gathering dust on staff's desks. At the end of term, there is a ritual clearing of desks, and there are no prizes for guessing where most of the stuff ends up! An overflowing desk is considered to demonstrate that its owner is very busy, while a clear desk is an invitation for more work to be placed on it. I disagree. If you have a pile of papers, you will waste minutes every time you have to go through it to find an item. You will be forced to glance at each item and divide it into smaller piles for immediate attention, later attention, and so on, and all this paper shuffling takes so long that all your free time is lost simply in thumbing through paper on your desk!

The best advice for dealing with paperwork is *do it now*. Don't put off dealing with small items. Of course, you will have priorities of lesson preparation and marking, but given these and your available free time, do make the effort to deal with matters as soon as possible. If you read something and then put the paper down, you will have to reread it later when you come to tackle it, so why not deal with it there and then? Try to make a rule only to read anything that falls on your desk *once*. If you can't settle the matter there and then, write down what you want to do, so that you don't need to start from scratch when you pick it up again. If there is no further action you can take at present, put it away in a pending file which you go through periodically to see what's happening. Don't leave pending items floating around your desk; you will keep picking them up unnecessarily and putting them back down again. Information items relating to a particular course can be put in your teaching file; other information should be filed in date order in a 'general' file, which you will need to clear out from time to time. The main thing is to keep your desk clear of endless clutter – other papers, such as advertising material, should be glanced at and then either disposed of at once or dealt with as above. For example, if it's a matter of filling in a form to ask for a textbook inspection copy, then get it done *now*; note the date you sent it off on the remainder of the publicity sheet, place it in your pending file, and send the form off. The secret is to keep the paper moving; the more you develop the habit of reading and dealing with it as soon as possible, the easier it will become.

COPING WITH MARKING

Those piles of marking will need to be handled efficiently, or the work of different classes will get muddled up. First, make sure every student puts his or her name on the top of each item submitted. Second, put all marking for a class straight into a folder of some sort. I use transparent plastic wallets, each with its colour-coded label for the class concerned. You shouldn't accumulate more than two or three full wallets on any one day – if you do, you haven't spread the 'due in' dates adequately for your own convenience. All you have to do then is to mark it, remembering that if you can do one class all at one sitting, you not only achieve greater consistency, but also save time spent on shifting papers, because you only have to assemble and put away all the documents once.

COPY MEMOS AND LETTERS

It's a good idea to keep copies of all memos and letters sent, and to see that someone has copies of all reports and references given. I also keep a note of when I make a report or reference for a student, with any grading given, just in case the original is temporarily mislaid, and I make the embarrassing mistake of giving a completely different grade the second time around!

USE OF THE TELEPHONE

Make good use of the telephone; it can be so much more flexible when dealing with difficult situations involving students, parents and employers. But make sure you take adequate notes of your conversations – it's tempting to think you'll remember all the details, but you don't usually, and what happens if you're off sick and a colleague has to take over? Don't skimp – take time to write up messages properly. Half the problems that arise in school and college staff rooms are caused by poor communications; don't add to them!

ASSISTANCE OF COLLEAGUES

One thing more: gaining the assistance of colleagues. Reports, references, collation of grades, exam meetings and course meetings, all involve the active cooperation of your colleagues. Inevitably, some will be better organized than others. If you are new to the staff room, and in a relatively junior position, you will have to adopt an appropriately diplomatic approach. However, you may have to go in for a bit of reminding and even nagging of colleagues who are slow in providing you with the information you need. Don't be afraid to ask senior staff to help you get the paperwork right; they will be much happier to assist you now, rather than after some awful administrative mess has been caused. So don't hesitate – if you're in a muddle with some aspect of administration or indeed any other matter, then *seek help* – don't wait until things get out of hand.

IMPORTANCE OF COPING WITH DATA

You will have appreciated from all this that a teacher – especially a full-time one – is rather like the central processor of a computer, having to assemble and process large quanitities of data, mostly concerning students. This may seem the least rewarding part of your job, but it is absolutely vital; if you don't master it, your students may suffer, but if you get it right, your teaching – and your students' learning – will benefit enormously.

Chapter 5

Achieving Job Satisfaction Through Relations with Students, Colleagues and the Outside World

You cannot teach a man anything; you can only help him to find it within himself.

Galileo

Teaching is a bit like farming: you can spend a lot of time toiling over rather unpromising material, but now and again you can stand back and think of the successes you have had, the fruits of your labour. I went into teaching because I didn't feel stretched in my previous job. I have never complained of that since entering this profession! But we still need some tangible job satisfaction, and in this chapter I try to show how it can be achieved through the new world of human relationships which opens up to teachers, and to which I referred at the beginning of my introduction to this book.

The Pastoral Care of Students

Even though in many countries the teacher is no longer the pillar of the community he or she once was, this does not alter the fact that we still have a responsibility to our students, which varies according to their age and the nature of their course. The pastoral care of students cannot just be left to special tutors, so recognize that you may have a part to play here. I have already strongly recommended that if you are having difficulties with any students, you should consult their course tutor or other senior member of staff. If *you* are the responsible person, bear in mind a few golden rules when dealing with students in a pastoral capacity.

WARNING SIGNALS
Warning signals are frequently noticed first by one of the ordinary subject teachers, through absence, inability to produce work set, or strange behaviour in class. These signals should be passed on to you, as course tutor, and likewise, you should inform other tutors of anything untoward which you notice as a subject teacher. You must then decide what to do, including what, if anything, should be put in writing on the student's papers. The best first step is to consult a senior member of staff, to get a second, and more experienced, opinion. Don't try to carry all your student problems on your own shoulders. These matters can take up an inordinate amount of your time, so do seek help before you become involved as a sort of part-time social worker.

LISTENING
Listening is about the most important thing you can do to assist a youngster, or indeed someone of any age, who has a problem. If you intend to make a career in teaching, you may wish to consider taking a proper course in counselling; one of the skills you will be taught is how to listen. Sometimes students wish to unburden

their problems on a teacher with whom they feel they have a certain empathy, probably because they are not on good terms with other persons to whom they might turn, such as their parents.

REFERRAL AND STAFF-ROOM SURGERIES

Referral to a more specialized counsellor or agency is essential if you uncover some deep-seated emotional trauma, or problems involving drugs, suicide or other serious matters. In many cases you can't force a student to seek this professional help, but you need to be aware that if you are untrained in counselling, you can soon get out of your depth. Indeed, it is not unknown for teachers to give well-meaning but erroneous advice to students seeking help in this context, so do not go beyond your area of competence here. You can listen sympathetically, certainly, and give a view on how the student's problem is affecting his or her studies, but don't become a self-appointed student counsellor without proper training.

Some schools offer a kind of staff-room surgery: a sort of 'open house' for students to come at certain times of the day to consult teachers over any problem connected with their studies. Since so many study problems are linked with other personal problems, this is a way of encouraging students to share their learning problems, with the opportunity for referral if required. Obviously, such an arrangement cannot be made by one teacher in isolation, but it does seem a good idea for getting students to appreciate their teachers' role as more than simply classroom performers.

RELATIONS WITH PARENTS

Relations with parents are crucial in all cases involving younger students, and even with those in the 16 – 20 age group. It is quite normal for a young person to have feelings of rebellion against authority in general and parents in particular, so do not be too impressed by the vicissitudes of the ordinary teenager. You will sometimes find yourself in the position of a mediator between students and parents. It's a well-known truism that you can't put an old head on young shoulders, so you have to do what you can to dispense impartial wisdom and common sense. If you have met the parents and established some sort of rapport with them, it will be that much easier to see both sides of the problem, and help with a little family reconciliation.

Relations with the Outside World

Much of what I have suggested for helping students involves the development of relations with people outside your school or college. Parents must come first on the list, and teachers conventionally make their acquaintance at student admittance interviews and then less formally at parents' evenings. A few tips for the latter: there is usually a queue to see you, so be brief and be well briefed – have all the facts about each student's progress at your fingertips. Note any relevant points made by the parents, otherwise you will never remember afterwards. Don't waffle and try to 'show off' in front of parents; be honest, concise, and realistic, because this will be of more assistance in the long run to a son or daughter than false words of praise to please the parents.

Increasingly, teachers are coming into contact with school and college governors as they become more involved with day-to-day operations. Your aim should be to build up good relationships with these people; your job will be much easier if there exists mutual respect. You can expect occasional visits from Her Majesty's Inspectors and other educational advisors; if you have adopted the professional approach to teaching I recommend, you will have nothing to fear. A similar approach will serve you well in dealings with social workers, since you are all trying to act in the best interests of the students concerned. Professional cooperation can be very fruitful; the problems arise when communications break down. Keep written notes of all meetings and discussions with persons outside your institution, and make sure that everything you need to do is done promptly and with the knowledge of your superiors.

Since a school or college is not an enclosed institution, we should take every opportunity to involve ourselves and our students in the outside world, remembering that learning is not the sole prerogative of educational institutions. Schools and colleges are taking a higher profile in the community, and each member of staff is an ambassador. Many older students now have a period of work experience as part of their course. This helps them to become familiar with the world of work, but it is also an opportunity for you to build up those vital links with local employers. You need to begin this as soon as you start to teach, because equipping students for life must involve some comprehension of local employment opportunities and the quality of life which they offer.

Seize every chance to invite employers and other representatives of 'the world outside' into your classroom. Don't rely too heavily on the traditional 'talk', but encourage a 'news conference' approach, with plenty of two-way communication. If necessary, get your students to prepare a set of questions in advance, to avoid those embarrassing silences. Having a list of people who can come in and put across fresh ideas to your students is worth a great deal; try to pick the natural communicators, who would have made good teachers!

You can also do your part to help external relations by seeing that your students behave themselves on outside visits. Through visits you can get students to see places which they would otherwise never go near; they will also come across helpful people such as museum curators who are only too willing to share their enthusiasm for a subject. With so much apathy and *ennui* around these days, it does young people good to be exposed to a little enthusiasm outside of the artificial educational environment. It is better still if the students can become personally involved, in the best 'doing' tradition of learning, perhaps providing some sort of voluntary community work, or raising funds for a local good cause. This will help both students and teachers to appreciate the value of their institution in the wider context of the community.

Relations with Colleagues

An educational institution is no different from other organizations to the extent that you will have to learn to cooperate with all manner of men and women. In my experience, teachers are generally helpful, caring human beings. They usually have particular sympathy for new teachers, and will go out of their way to help. I use the word 'sympathy' deliberately, because they know that some of the new teacher's idealistic notions will be rapidly dispelled by the harsh reality of the teaching environment. It is as important to cultivate the friendship of your colleagues as it is to earn the respect of your students. Although much of a teacher's work may be done as a solo performance, the delivery of a course normally depends on a number of teachers working together. You need to build up a reputation for contributing your fair share of the effort required for this purpose, so that your track record will eventually justify the reward of promotion to a position of greater responsibility.

We have all been on the receiving end of education in our youth, but if you are now entering the teaching profession, you may be apprehensive about the welcome that awaits you from your new colleagues. Let me put your mind at rest; teachers are very tolerant of their colleagues, especially if they are inexperienced. Provided that you are obviously trying to do your best, no experienced teacher is going to complain about the problems you may cause during your first years of teaching. It is said that doctors bury their mistakes, but teachers have to accept theirs and go on facing their students and working with their colleagues. The only way that you will lose the friendship of your colleagues is if they perceive that you are not pulling your weight, but relying on the excuse of newness to the profession.

Teaching is such a responsible job that your colleagues may often seem to have their minds elsewhere when you meet them. They are probably planning in their heads their next-lesson-but-one, or mulling over some problem student. As the term progresses, don't be put off by their expressions of world-weariness; remember that teachers have to give a lot, so that by the end of term they may well be emotionally drained as well as physically exhausted. They will welcome your fresh approach to the job, but won't be impressed if you imply that they are all burnt out. Experience counts for a great deal in teaching, so respect those who have been in the profession much longer than you; better still, learn from them!

Achieving Job Satisfaction

Most new teachers find the job very fulfilling for the first few years, as they master new techniques and achieve their first learning successes. You will be too busy to worry about where it is all leading; the sense of achievement in becoming a proficient teacher is reward enough. There may come a day, however, when you begin to wonder whether you are still experiencing any *real* job satisfaction. A variety of reasons may account for this situation, but often it comes down to the simple matter of recognition. You feel that your efforts have not been recognized by those in authority. This makes a few teachers very resentful, while some others simply retreat into their subject and take very little part in the corporate life of their school or college. There's no doubt in my mind that the contribution of teachers to the community is not fully recognized and therefore undervalued by society, but as I stated in the introduction, teaching should be a vocation; you don't leave a vocation unless forced to by economic necessity. The employment opportunities outside teaching appear peculiarly attractive to teachers; some jobs are easier, of course, but some are harder. The real point is that other jobs are *different*, and you have to decide whether the alternatives will offer you equal satisfaction, albeit in a different form.

I always think it sad that someone who has trained as a teacher, and gathered experience, should find it necessary to quit the profession. If you are just embarking on your teaching career, I would like to warn you that you too may have doubts after a few years, and may well be tempted to give up. Your working conditions and remuneration may be poor, your students unresponsive, and your superiors unsympathetic. Above all, you may feel stale and listless, with your early idealism seemingly gone forever. When you reach this stage, the moment has come to take stock of your teaching career. In my opinion, there are very few teachers who do not have quite a lot to offer their students. If you leave teaching, you deprive these students of your experience. The wealth of human relationships that you build up among students and staff cannot quickly be reinstated by a replacement; institutions with a high rate of staff turnover are not noted for educational success.

Two pieces of advice may help you face any 'mid-career crisis' and overcome it. First, appreciate that a common early symptom is irritability, both with students and colleagues. As a general rule, a calm teacher is more effective than a highly emotional one. There will be many occasions when your nerves may be put on edge: some students are very wearing, and may even deliberately try to 'wind you up'; colleagues may let you down; the authorities may appear to be inconsiderate and dictatorial; and parents and employers may fail to appreciate your efforts. Usually, these irritations come down to personalities, and my advice is not to let these people get under your skin. This is especially true of any particular students who irritate you. Try to remain professional, showing no vindictiveness to these thorns in your side, but neither letting them spoil your teaching. Try to understand that your health is more important than any petty annoyances that they may cause, so don't let them ruin your career. Take a deep breath and dismiss them from your mind; concentrate on the learning of the majority of your students, and don't be deflected by the ingratitude of a few. If you are regularly in a 'wound up' state, seek help with relaxation techniques; there are some good 'self-help' books available. Another sensible idea is to have a hobby in which you can immerse yourself in your spare time; this presupposes that you have some, but you may be doing yourself a favour if you 'make' time to pursue a leisure interest that helps to refresh and reinvigorate you.

My second piece of advice is that you must pace *yourself* as well as your lessons. When you are new to teaching, you may want to keep up a tremendous pace of giving out to your students for week after week. However, you soon come to realize that if you continue in this fashion, you will rapidly burn yourself out. More experienced teachers may appear to be coasting a little, but it's more likely that they are conserving energy to stay the course. So try to appreciate this yourself and adjust your pace accordingly. Emulate great actors; they pace their performance, always holding something in reserve. If you don't do this, your own reserves of nervous energy may run out in mid-career, to the detriment of both you and your students.

There's no doubt that teaching is an endurance test; you must brace yourself for a relentless grind during term time, always trying to keep up with marking, lesson preparation and administrative tasks – no wonder that teachers look forward to the holidays even more than their students do! This is the *reality* of teaching, which you must face up to when your initial enthusiasm for the job begins to evaporate. You *can* face up to this successfully if you understand that your students' learning is usually a slow, steady process; the teacher who can accept this and patiently endure the long haul will be rewarded. If you adopt the techniques I advocate, you will find that as you become more experienced, you don't have to make such an exhausting input into each lesson; you should be able to judge exactly how much you need to put into a lesson to bring about effective learning. The trick is to *enhance* your students' input, so that better learning is achieved through a student-centred rather than a teacher-centred approach. If you can become a learning consultant and facilitator rather than just a teacher, this should ensure that you can retain some of your energy and most of your enthusiasm for this most rewarding of professions.

Full Circle

Much of what has been touched upon in this chapter, and indeed the whole book, is concerned with the emerging role of the teacher as learning consultant rather than simply a communicator of skills and knowledge. You remain the facilitator, the prime mover for learning, but you begin to provide your students with the power – and it is power indeed – not to need a teacher, but to be self-motivated, self-critical, in short, committed to learning for themselves. This is the true vocation of all teachers; a goal to be aimed for through our influence over the students entrusted to us.

Sometimes, we can sense that our influence has had a decisive effect on a young person's development, although this is rare. More often we will have been one of a series of influences – some good, some bad – which help to mould our students' characters. If you think that we, as teachers, have little influence on our students, recall your own days at school or college. Do you remember your teachers fairly clearly, even from primary school upwards? I believe most of us do, and that the influence of teachers is both profound and long lasting. As a teacher, you are dealing with human beings at the most impressionable time of their lives, and there you are, standing before them as a model. Younger students especially may copy or adapt certain aspects of your behaviour, and pick up your hopes, fears and prejudices, for good or ill. What a great responsibility! Many young eyes will be upon you; remember that you probably teach as much by what you don't say and do, as by what you are trying to communicate; it's the *example* that you give which matters. Students take more notice of a popular, respected and admired teacher, so if we aspire to be like this, we know that the learning of our students will also benefit.

So now we have come full circle, because I began Chapter 1 by pointing out the example we must set our students in our lives both inside and outside the classroom. Of course, we receive so little thanks from the objects of our efforts that we are often misled into believing that much of the seed we sow falls upon stoney ground, and so it might seem at the time. But never underestimate the potential for that small seed to come to life at some later date, and bear fruit in a way of which we shall never be aware. It is all rather trite to proclaim that we are equipping the next few generations, but we do have a central role in this awesome task, along with parents and the other members of society with whom our students have regular contact. The trouble is that these fine sentiments have to be translated into the everyday grind of teaching. It's easy to wax lyrical about teaching when you are savouring some pedagogic points in a teaching practice seminar, but when you are facing some ramshackle class of poorly motivated teenagers on a Friday afternoon, your feelings will, I warrant, be less well disposed towards the profession.

What is to be done? Teaching, like most worthwhile human activities, involves sacrifices: investment of time and energy for a reward in terms of job satisfaction which is neither guaranteed nor often enjoyed directly. If you are new to teaching, or have some experience but are hoping this book can help you recharge your batteries, I can only say that I have tried to share some of my own thoughts and experiences. Ultimately, of course, you must look *within yourself* for the enthusiasm which will provide you with the ability to make your career in teaching a successful one. Good luck!